# THE
# LITTLE
# VIRTUES

Books by Natalia Ginzburg

*All Our Yesterdays*

*Family Sayings*

*The Little Virtues*

*The City and the House*

*The Manzoni Family*

*Valentino and Sagittarius*

*Family: Family and Borghesia,
  Two Novellas*

*Voices in the Evening*

# THE
# LITTLE
# VIRTUES

*Translated from the Italian*
*by Dick Davis*

## NATALIA GINZBURG

ARCADE PUBLISHING • NEW YORK

Originally published in Italy under the title *Le Piccole Virtù*.

Arcade Publishing books may be purchased in bulk at special discounts
for sales promotion, corporate gifts, fund-raising, or educational
purposes. Special editions can also be created to specifications. For
details, contact the Special Sales Department, Arcade Publishing, 307
West 36th Street, 11th Floor, New York, NY 10018 or
arcade@skyhorsepublishing.com.

Arcade Publishing® is a registered trademark of
Skyhorse Publishing, Inc.®, a Delaware corporation.

Visit our website at www.arcadepub.com.

10 9 8 7 6 5 4 3 2 1

Library of Congress Cataloging-in-Publication Data
is available on file.

ISBN: 978-1-61145-797-1

Printed in the United States of America

# CONTENTS

Foreword

# FOREWORD

The essays collected here appeared in various newspapers and magazines. I am grateful to these newspapers and magazines for permission to reprint them.

They were written at the following times in the following places:

Winter in the Abruzzi (*Inverno in Abruzzo*), written in Rome in the autumn of 1944, published in *Aretusa*; Worn-out Shoes (*Le scarpe rotte*), written in Rome in the autumn of 1945, published in *Politecnico*; Portrait of a Friend (*Ritratto d'un amico*), written in Rome in 1957, appeared in *Radiocorriere*; England: Eulogy and Lament (*Elogio e compianto dell'Inghilterra*), written in London in the spring of 1961, published in *Mondo*; La Maison Volpé (*La Maison Volpé*), written in London in the spring of 1960, published in *Mondo*; He and I (*Lui e io*), written in Rome in the summer of 1962, and I think unpublished; The Son of Man (*Il Figlio dell'uomo*), written in Turin in 1946, published in *Unità*; My Vocation (*Il mio mestiere*), written in Turin in the autumn of 1949, published in *Ponte*; Silence (*Silenzio*), written in Turin in 1951, published in *Cultura e realtà*; Human Relationships (*I rapporti umani*), written in Rome in the spring of 1953, published in *Terza Generazione*; The Little Virtues (*Le piccole virtú*), written in London in the spring of 1960, and published in *Nuovi Argomenti*.

The dates are significant because they account for the changes in style. I have corrected virtually none of these essays because I am only able to correct what I write at the time that I am writing it. When this time has passed I don't know how to make corrections. And so this book perhaps does not have much uniformity of style, and I apologise for this.

I dedicate this book to a friend of mine, whose name I shall not mention. He is not present in any of these essays, nevertheless he is the person to whom most of them are secretly addressed. Many of these essays would not have been written if I had not had various conversations with him. He gave a legitimacy and freedom of expression to certain things I had been turning over in my mind.

I record my affection and great friendship for him here — a friendship which, like all real friendships, has passed through the fire of violent disagreements.

# Part One

# Winter in the Abruzzi

*God has given us this moment of peace*

There are only two seasons in the Abruzzi: summer
and winter. The spring is snowy and windy like the
winter, and the autumn is hot and clear like the summer.
Summer starts in June and ends in November. The long
days of sunshine on the low, parched hills, the yellow
dust in the streets and the babies' dysentery come to an
end, and winter begins. People stop living in the streets:
the barefoot children disappear from the church steps. In
the region I am talking about almost all the men
disappeared after the last crops were brought in: they
went for work to Terni, Sulmona or Rome. Many
bricklayers came from that area, and some of the houses
were elegantly built; they were like small villas with
terraces and little columns, and when you entered them
you would be astonished to find large dark kitchens with
hams hanging from the ceilings, and vast, dirty, empty
rooms. In the kitchen a fire would be burning, and there
were various kinds of fire: there were great fires of oak
logs, fires of branches and leaves, fires of twigs picked up
one by one in the street. It was easier to tell the rich from
the poor by looking at the fires they burnt than by
looking at the houses or at the people themselves, or at
their clothes and shoes which were all more or less the
same.

When I first arrived in that countryside all the faces
looked the same to me, all the women — rich and poor,
young and old — resembled one another. Almost all of
them had toothless mouths: exhaustion and a wretched
diet, the unremitting overwork of childbirth and breast
feeding, mean that women lose their teeth there when

they are thirty. But then, gradually, I began to distin-
guish Vincenzina from Secondina, Annunziata from
Addolerata, and I began to go into their houses and warm
myself at their various fires.

When the first snows began to fall a quiet sadness took
hold of us. We were in exile: our city was a long way off,
and so were books, friends, the various desultory events
of a real existence. We lit our green stove with its long
chimney that went through the ceiling: we gathered
together in the room with the stove — there we cooked
and ate, my husband wrote at the big oval table, the
children covered the floor with toys. There was an eagle
painted on the ceiling of the room, and I used to look at
the eagle and think that was exile. Exile was the eagle, the
murmur of the green stove, the vast, silent countryside
and the motionless snow. At five o'clock the bell of the
church of Santa Maria would ring and the women with
their black shawls and red faces went to Benediction.
Every evening my husband and I went for a walk: every
evening we walked arm in arm, sinking our feet into the
snow. The houses that ran alongside the street were lived
in by people we knew and liked, and they all used to
come to the door to greet us. Sometimes one would ask,
'When will you go back to your own house?' My
husband answered, 'When the war is over'. 'And when
will this war be over? You know everything and you're a
professor, when will it be over?' They called my husband
'the professor' because they could not pronounce his
name, and they came from a long way off to ask his
advice on the most diverse things · — the best season for
having teeth out, the subsidies which the town-hall gave,
and the different taxes and duties.

In winter when an old person died of pneumonia the
bell of Santa Maria sounded the death knell and Domenico Orecchia, the joiner, made the coffin. A woman
went mad and they took her to the lunatic asylum at
Collemaggio, and this was the talk of the countryside for

a while. She was a young, clean woman, the cleanest in the whole district; they said it was excessive cleanliness that had done it to her. Girl twins were born to Gigetto di Calcedonio who already had boy twins, and there was a row at the town-hall because the authorities did not want to give the family any help as they had quite a bit of land and an immense kitchen-garden. A neighbour spat in the eye of Rosa, the school caretaker, and she went about with her eye bandaged because she intended to pay back the insult. 'The eye is a delicate thing, and spit is salty,' she explained. And this was talked about for a while, until there was nothing else to say about it.

Every day homesickness grew in us. Sometimes it was even pleasant, like being in gentle slightly intoxicating company. Letters used to arrive from our city with news of marriages and deaths from which we were excluded. Sometimes our homesickness was sharp and bitter, and turned into hatred; then we hated Domenico Orecchia, Gigetto di Calcedonio, Annunziatina, the bells of Santa Maria. But it was a hatred which we kept hidden because we knew it was unjust; and our house was always full of people who came to ask for favours and to offer them. Sometimes the dressmaker made a special kind of dumpling for us. She would wrap a cloth round her waist and beat the eggs, and send Crocetta around the countryside to see if she could borrow a really big saucepan. Her red face was absorbed in her work and her eyes shone with a proud determination. She would have burnt the house down to make her dumplings come out a success. Her clothes and hair became white with flour and then she would place the dumplings with great care on the oval table where my husband wrote.

Crocetta was our serving woman. In fact she was not a woman because she was only fourteen years old. It was the dressmaker who had found her. The dressmaker divided the world into two groups — those who comb their hair and those who do not comb their hair. It was necessary to be on the lookout against those who do not comb their hair because, naturally, they have lice. Crocetta combed her hair; and so she came to work for us and tell our children long stories about death and cemeteries. Once upon a time there was a little boy whose mother died. His father chose another wife and this stepmother didn't love the little boy. So she killed him when his father was out in the fields, and she boiled him in a stew. His father came home for supper, but, after he had finished eating, the bones that were left on the plate started to sing

> Mummy with an angry frown
> Popped me in the cooking pot,
> When I was done and piping hot
> Greedy daddy gulped me down.

Then the father killed his wife with a scythe and he hung her from a nail in front of the door. Sometimes I find myself murmuring the words of the song in the story, and then the whole country is in front of me again, together with the particular atmosphere of its seasons, its yellow gusting wind and the sound of its bells.

Every morning I went out with my children and there was a general amazed disapproval that I should expose them to the cold and the snow. 'What sin have the poor creatures committed?' people said. 'This isn't the time for walking, dear. Go back home.' I went for long walks in the white deserted countryside, and the few people I met looked at the children with pity. 'What sin have they committed?' they said to me. There, if a baby is born in winter they do not take it out of the room until the summer comes. At midday my husband used to catch me up with the post and we went back to the house together.

I talked to the children about our city. They had been very small when we left, and had no memories of it at all. I told them that there the houses had many storeys, that there were so many houses and so many streets, and so many big fine shops. 'But here there is Giro's,' the children said.

Giro's shop was exactly opposite our house. Giro used to stand in the doorway like an old owl, gazing at the street with his round, indifferent eyes. He sold a bit of everything; groceries and candles, postcards, shoes and oranges. When the stock arrived and Giro unloaded the crates, boys ran to eat the rotten oranges that he threw away. At Christmas nougat, liqueurs and sweets also arrived. But he never gave the slightest discount on his prices. 'How mean you are, Giro,' the women said to him, and he answered 'People who aren't mean get eaten by dogs'. At Christmas the men returned from Terni, Sulmona and Rome, stayed for a few days, and set off again after they had slaughtered the pigs. For a few days people ate nothing but *sfrizzoli*, incredible sausages that made you drink the whole time; and then the squeal of the new piglets would fill the street.

In February the air was soft and damp. Grey, swollen clouds travelled across the sky. One year during the thaw the gutters broke. Then water began to pour into the house and the rooms became a veritable quagmire. But it was like this throughout the whole area; not one house remained dry. The women emptied buckets out of their windows and swept the water out of their front doors. There were people who went to bed with an open umbrella. Domenico Orecchia said that it was a punishment for some sin. This lasted for a week; then, at last, every trace of snow disappeared from the roofs, and Aristide mended the gutters.

A restlessness awoke in us as winter drew to its end. Perhaps someone would come to find us: perhaps something would finally happen. Our exile had to have an end too. The roads which separated us from the world seemed shorter; the post arrived more often. All our chilblains gradually got better.

There is a kind of uniform monotony in the fate of

man. Our lives unfold according to ancient, unchange-
able laws, according to an invariable and ancient rhythm.
Our dreams are never realized and as soon as we see them
betrayed we realize that the intensest joys of our life have
nothing to do with reality. No sooner do we see them
betrayed than we are consumed with regret for the time
when they glowed within us. And in this succession of
hopes and regrets our life slips by.

My husband died in Rome, in the prison of Regina
Coeli, a few months after we left the Abruzzi. Faced with
the horror of his solitary death, and faced with the
anguish which preceded his death, I ask myself if this
happened to us — to us, who bought oranges at Giro's
and went for walks in the snow. At that time I believed in
a simple and happy future, rich with hopes that were
fulfilled, with experiences and plans that were shared.
But that was the best time of my life, and only now that
it has gone from me forever — only now do I realize it.

# Worn-Out Shoes

My shoes are worn out, and the friend I live with at the moment also has worn-out shoes. When we are together we often talk about shoes. If I talk about the time when I shall be an old, famous writer, she immediately asks me 'What shoes will you wear?' Then I say I shall have shoes made of green suede with a big gold buckle on one side.

I belong to a family in which everyone has sound, solid shoes. My mother possessed so many pairs of shoes that she even had to have a little wardrobe made especially for them. Whenever I visit them they utter cries of indignation and sorrow at the sight of my shoes. But I know that it is possible to live even with worn-out shoes. During the German occupation I was alone here in Rome, and I only had one pair of shoes. If I had taken them to the cobbler's I would have had to stay in bed for two or three days, and in my situation that was impossible. So I continued to wear them and when — on top of everything else — it rained, I felt them gradually falling apart, becoming soft and shapeless, and I felt the coldness of the pavement beneath the soles of my feet. This is why I still wear worn-out shoes, because I remember that particular pair and compared with them my present shoes don't seem too bad; besides, if I have money I would rather spend it on something else as shoes don't seem to me to be very essential things. When I was young I was always surrounded by tender, solicitous affection and I was spoilt, but that year when I was here in Rome I was alone for the first time and this is why I like Rome so much — even though it is full of history for me, full of terrible memories and very few hours of happiness. My friend also has worn-out shoes, and this is why we get on well together. My friend has no one to reproach her about the shoes she wears, she has only a brother who lives in the country and goes around in hunting boots. She and I know what happens when it rains, and your bare legs get soaked and the water comes into your shoes, so that there is a slight sound — a kind of soft squelch — at every step.

My friend has a pale, masculine face and when she smokes she uses a black cigarette holder. The first time that I saw her, seated at a table, with her tortoise-shell rimmed spectacles and her mysterious, haughty face, with the black cigarette-holder gripped between her teeth, I thought she looked like a Chinese general. At that time I did not know that she had worn-out shoes. I discovered this later.

We have only known each other a few months, but it seems as many years. My friend has no children; I, on the other hand, do have children and to her this is odd. She has never seen them, except in a photograph, because they live in the provinces with my mother, and this too — that she has never seen my children — is very odd for both of us. In one sense she has no problems, she can give in to the temptation to let her life go to pieces; I, on the other hand, cannot. So, my children live with my mother and so far they do not have worn-out shoes. But what kind of men will they be? I mean, what kind of shoes will they have when they are men? What road will they choose to walk down? Will they decide to give up everything that is pleasant but not necessary, or will they affirm that everything is necessary and that men have the right to wear sound, solid shoes on their feet?

My friend and I talk about this a great deal, and about how the world will be when I am an old, famous writer and she will go wandering through the world with a rucksack on her back like an old Chinese general, and my children will go along their road with sound, solid shoes and the firm step of someone who doesn't give up, or with worn-out shoes and the slow, dragging step of someone who understands what is not necessary.

Sometimes we arrange marriages between my children and the children of her brother, the one who goes around the country in hunting boots. We talk like this until the small hours of the night and drink black, bitter tea. We have a mattress and a bed, and every evening we toss up for which of the two of us shall sleep in the bed. When we get up in the morning our worn-out shoes are waiting for us on the rug.

Now and again my friend says that she is fed up with working and wants to let her life go to pieces. She wants to shut herself in some filthy bar and drink all her savings, or she will just stay in bed and think of nothing and leave everything to drift, and let them come and cut off the gas and the light. She says she will do it when I leave. Because our shared life will not last much longer; soon I shall leave and return to my mother and children and be in a house where no one is allowed to have worn-out shoes. My mother will take me in hand; she will stop me using pins instead of buttons and writing till the small hours. And, in my turn, I shall take my children in hand and overcome the temptation to let my life go to pieces. I shall become serious and motherly, as always happens when I am with them, a different person from the one I am now — a person my friend does not know at all.

I shall watch the clock and keep track of time, I shall be cautious and wary about everything and I shall take care that my children's feet are always warm and dry, as I know that they must be if it is at all possible — at least during infancy. And perhaps even for learning to walk in worn-out shoes, it is as well to have dry, warm feet when we are children.

# Portrait of a Friend

The city which our friend loved is always the same; there have been changes, but very few — they have introduced trolley buses and made one or two subways. There are no new cinemas. The ancient monuments are always there with their familiar names, which when we repeat them awaken in us our youth and childhood. Now, we live elsewhere in a completely different, much bigger city, and if we meet and talk about our own city we do so with no sense of regret that we have left it, and say that we could not live there any longer. But when we go back, simply passing through the station and walking in the misty avenues is enough to make us feel we have come home; and the sadness with which the city fills us every time we return lies in this feeling that we are at home and, at the same time, that we have no reason to stay here; because here, in our own home, our own city, the city in which we spent our youth, so few things remain alive for us and we are oppressed by a throng of memories and shadows.

Besides, our city is by its nature a melancholy place. On winter mornings it has its own smell of the station and soot, diffused through all its streets and avenues; if we arrive in the morning we find it grey with fog, pervaded by that distinctive smell. Sometimes a pale sun filters through the fog and dyes the heaps of snow and bare tree branches rose and lilac; in the streets and avenues the snow is shovelled into little heaps, but the parks are still buried beneath their thick, undisturbed blanket which lies, a finger thick, on the deserted benches and round the fountain rims: the clock by the horse track is stopped at a quarter to eleven, as it has been since time immemorial. There is a hill on the other side of the river and that too is white with snow, but marked here and there with reddish bushes; on the top of the hill a circular, orange-coloured building which used to be the Balilla National Opera stands like a tower. If there is a little sun to catch the glass dome of the Automobile Showrooms and make the river flow with a green glitter beneath its stone bridges, the city can seem, for a moment, pleasant and friendly; but that is a fleeting impression. The city's essential nature is melancholy; the river loses itself in the distance and disappears in a horizon of violet mists which make you think of sunsets at midday, and at any moment you can breathe in that same dark, industrial smell of soot, and hear the whistle of the trains.

And now it occurs to us that our city resembles the friend whom we have lost and who loved it; it is, as he was, industrious, stamped with a frown of stubborn, feverish activity; and it is simultaneously listless and inclined to spend its time idly dreaming. Wherever we go in the city that resembles him we feel that our friend lives again; on every corner and at every turning it seems that we could suddenly see his tall figure in its dark half-belted coat, his face hidden by the collar, his hat pulled down over his eyes. Stubborn and solitary our friend walked with his long tread throughout the city; he hid himself away in remote, smoky cafés where he would immediately slip off his coat and hat but keep on the pale, ugly scarf that was carelessly flung about his neck; he twisted strands of his long brown hair around his fingers and then, quick as lightning, pushed the strands back. He filled page after page with his quick, broad handwriting, crossing out furiously as he went; and in his poetry he celebrated the city,

> Questo è il giorno che salgono le nebbie dal fiume
> Nella bella città, in mezzo a prati e colline,
> E la sfumano come un ricordo . . .

[This is the day when mists rise from the river
In the beautiful city set among meadows and hills,
And they make it shadowy as a memory . . .]

When we return to the city or when we think of it his
poems echo in our ears; and we no longer know whether
they are good poems or not, because they have become
so much a part of us, and so strongly reflect for us the
image of our youth, of those far off days when we heard
them for the first time recited by the living voice of our
friend, and we discovered with astonishment that it is
possible to make poetry even out of our grey, heavy,
unpoetic city.

Our friend lived in the city as an adolescent, and he
lived in the same way until the end. His days were
extremely long and full of time, like an adolescent's; he
knew how to find time to study and to write, to earn his
living and to wander idly through the streets he loved;
whereas we, who staggered from laziness to frantic
activity and back again, wasted our time trying to decide
whether we were lazy or industrious. For many years he
did not want to submit to office hours or accept a definite
job; but when he did agree to sit behind a desk in an office
he became a meticulous employee and a tireless worker:
even so, he set aside an ample margin of free time for
himself — his meals were quickly over, he ate very little
and never slept.

At times he was very unhappy, but for a long time we
thought that he would be cured of this unhappiness when
he decided to become an adult; his unhappiness seemed
like that of a boy — the absent-minded, voluptuous
melancholy of a boy who has not yet got his feet on the
ground and who lives in the sterile, solitary world of his
dreams.

Sometimes, during the evening, he would come in
search of us; then he just sat, pale, with his scarf about his
neck, twisting strands of hair around his fingers or
crumpling a piece of paper; throughout the whole

evening he would not say a single word, or answer any of our questions. Suddenly, at last, he would snatch up his overcoat and leave. Then we were ashamed and asked ourselves if our company had disappointed him, if he had hoped to cheer himself up by being with us and been unsuccessful; or perhaps he had simply wanted to spend an evening in silence beneath a lamp that was not his own.

However, conversation with him was never easy, even when he seemed happy; but a meeting with him in which just a few words were exchanged could be far more stimulating than with anyone else. In his company we became more intelligent; we felt compelled to articulate whatever was best and most serious in us, and we got rid of commonplace notions, imprecise thoughts, incoherent ideas.

We often felt ashamed when we were with him, because we did not know how to be serious like him, or modest like him, or generous and unselfish like him. He treated us, who were his friends, in a brusque way and he did not overlook any of our faults; but if we were upset or ill he immediately became as solicitous as a mother. On principle he refused to get to know new people; but sometimes he would be expansive and affectionate, full of appointments and plans, with someone completely unexpected — someone who was even rather contemptible — and whom he had never seen before. If we happened to remark that this person was in many ways unpleasant or despicable he used to say he was well aware of that, because he always liked to know everything and never allowed us the satisfaction of telling him something new: but he never explained why he acted in such a welcoming, intimate way with this person and, on the other hand, refused his friendship to others who deserved it much more, and we never discovered the reason. From time to time he became curious about someone who, he thought, was very elegant, and he would see a great deal of this person; perhaps he thought he could use these people in his novels; but he was mistaken in his judgements of social refinement and he often mistook bottle-glass for crystal; in this, but only in this, he was very naïve. But though he made mistakes about social refinement no one could deceive him when it came to spiritual or cultural refinement.

He had a cautious, reserved way of shaking hands — a few fingers were extended and withdrawn; a secretive, parsimonious way of taking his tobacco from its pouch and filling his pipe; and if he knew that we needed money he had a sudden, brusque way of giving it to us — so brusque and sudden that we were left rather bewildered; he used to say that he felt he should be careful with the money he had and that it hurt him to part with it, but once it was gone he didn't give a damn about it. If we were separated from him he neither wrote to us nor answered our letters, or he answered with a few, flat, defensive phrases; he said the reason was that he did not know how to feel affection for friends when they were a long way off; he did not want to suffer because of their absence and he quickly buried the thought of them.

He never had a wife or children or a house of his own. He lived with a married sister who loved him and whom he loved, but when he was with his family he behaved in his usual uncouth way and his manners were those of a boy or a stranger. Sometimes he came to our houses and then he would scrutinize the children we were bringing up, the families we had made for ourselves, with a puzzled, good-natured frown: he too thought of having a family but he thought of it in a way which with the passing of the years became more and more complicated and tortuous — so tortuous that it was impossible for him to bring the idea to a simple conclusion. Over the years he had built up such a tangled and inexorable system of ideas and principles that he was unable to carry through the simplest project, and the more forbidden and impossible he made the attainment of some simple reality the deeper his desire to master it became, twining itself in ever more complicated tangles like some suffocating species of vegetation. For this reason he was often unhappy and we would have liked to help him, but he never allowed us to utter a word of pity or make any gesture of sympathy; we even imitated his behaviour and refused his sympathy when we were depressed. Although he taught us many things he was not a mentor for us because we saw all too clearly the absurd convolutions of the thoughts in which he imprisoned his simple nature; we wanted to teach him something too — how to live in a more elementary, less suffocating way. But we were never able to teach him anything, because as soon as we tried to set out our arguments he would lift his hand and say that he was already well aware of all that.

In his last years his face was lined and furrowed, laid waste by mental torment; but his build and figure retained their adolescent gracefulness to the end. In his last years he became a famous writer but this had no effect at all on his secretive habits, nor on the modesty of his behaviour, nor on the scrupulous humility with which he carried out his everyday work. When we asked him if he enjoyed being famous he gave a proud smirk and said that he had always expected to be; sometimes a shrewd, proud smirk — childish and spiteful — used to flash across his face and disappear. But because he had always expected it, it gave him no pleasure when it came, since as soon as he had something he was incapable of loving or enjoying it.

He used to say that he knew his art so thoroughly that it was impossible he should discover any further secret in it, and because it could not promise him any more secrets it no longer interested him. He told us, who were his friends, that we had no more secrets for him and that we bored him profoundly; we felt humiliated by the fact that we bored him but we were unable to tell him that we saw only too clearly where his mistake lay — in his refusal to love the daily current of existence which flows on evenly and apparently without secrets. He had not as yet mastered day to day reality, but this — for which he felt a simultaneous desire and disgust — was impregnable and forbidden to him; and so he could only look at it as if from an infinite distance.

He died in the summer. In summer our city is deserted and seems very large, clear and echoing, like an empty city-square; the sky has a milky pallor, limpid but not luminous; the river flows as level as a street and gives off neither humidity nor freshness. Sudden clouds of dust rise from the streets; huge carts loaded with sand pass by on their way from the river; the asphalt of the main avenue is littered with pebbles that bake in the tar. Outside the cafés, beneath their fringed umbrellas, the little tables are deserted and red-hot.

None of us were there. He chose to die on an ordinary, stiflingly hot day in August, and he chose a room in a hotel near the station; he wanted to die like a stranger in the city to which he belonged. He had imagined his death in a poem written many, many years before:

> Non sara necessario lasciare il letto.
> Solo l'alba entrerà nella stanza vuota.
> Basterà la finestra a vestire ogni cosa
> D'un chiarore tranquillo, quasi una luce.
> Poserà un'ombra scarna sul volto supino.
> I ricordi saranno dei grumi d'ombra
> Appiattati cosí come vecchia brace
> Nel camino. Il ricordo sarà la vampa
> Che ancor ieri mordeva negli occhi spenti.

> [It will not be necessary to get up from the bed.
> Only the morning will enter the empty room.
> The window will be sufficient to clothe everything
> With a quiet clarity, like a light.
> It will cast a thin shadow on his face where it lies.
> What will be remembered are clots of shadow
> Flattened like old ashes

In the fireplace. Memory will be the flame
That yesterday flared in his dead eyes.]

A short time after his death we went on a trip into the hills. There were inns by the roadside with pergolas covered in ripening grapes, games of bowls, heaps of bicycles; there were farms growing corn cobs, and cut grass spread out on sacks to dry; it was the landscape just beyond the city, at the end of autumn, which he loved. We watched the September night come up over the low hills and ploughed fields. We were all close friends and had known each other for many years, we were people who had always worked and thought together. As happens among those who have suffered a misfortune together we tried to love each other all the more, to look after and protect each other; because we felt that he, in some mysterious way of his own, had always looked after us and protected us. On that hillside he was more present than ever.

Ogni occhiata che torna, conserva un gusto
Di erba e cose impregnate di sole a sera
Sulla spiaggia. Conserva un fiato di mare.
Come un mare notturno è quest'ombra vaga
Di ansie e brividi antichi, che il cielo sfiora
E ogni sera ritorna. Le voci morte
Assomigliano al frangersi di quel mare.

[As it comes back, every glance keeps some quality
Of the grass and of the things on the beach
Suffused by the evening sun. It keeps a breath of the sea.
This indistinct shadow compounded of anxieties
And ancient shudderings is like a nocturnal sea
On which the sky rests lightly, and which
Returns each evening. The voices of the dead
Are like the breaking of that sea.]

# England: Eulogy and Lament

England is beautiful and melancholy. To be honest I don't know many countries, but I begin to suspect that England is the most melancholy country in the world.

It is an extremely civilized country. There the basic problems of life — sickness, old age, unemployment, taxes have apparently been wisely solved.

It is a country which, I believe, knows how to govern itself well and this is clear in the smallest details of daily life.

It is a country where the greatest respect for others is a general and willingly observed rule.

It is a country which has always shown itself ready to welcome foreigners, from very diverse communities, without I think oppressing them.

It is a country where they know how to build houses. A man's wish to be snug in his own little house, which is just for him and his family, and to have a garden which he cultivates himself, is considered quite reasonable, and so the cities are made up of just such little houses.

Even the most ordinary houses look charming from the outside.

And a huge city like London, which is of a monstrous size, is organized in such a way that you do not realize how large it is and so you are not troubled by it. The eye is not bewildered by immensity but attracted and beguiled by the little streets, the little houses and the green parks.

The parks appear in the city like lakes — your eyes rest there, refreshed and at ease, cleansed of soot.

Because wherever the city is not green it is quickly smothered in a thick blanket of soot and smells like a railway station — of old trains, dust and coal.

The railway stations are the places where England is most openly gloomy. Scrap iron piles up there and coal dust and heaps of rusting, tangled, disused rails. They are surrounded by desolate little allotments full of cabbages, where bits of underwear are hung out to dry and where there are sheds patched together like old sheets.

The suburbs of London, where the streets of little identical houses go on and on in a way that makes you feel dizzy, are also extremely gloomy.

Here in London the sight of some shop-windows filled to overflowing with shoes that all have the same pointed toes and stiletto heels makes me feel equally dizzy. Or windows brimming over with women's underclothes — so stuffed with merchandise that my eyes feel sated with it and any desire to buy a slip or a pair of stockings is completely destroyed. To see such abundance gives me the impression that I don't need anything at all, and I feel a revulsion against stockings and slips that seems as though it will last for ever.

The small new leaves are a tender green on the trees and stand out like delicate embroidery against the red-brick walls of the little houses.

From time to time on the street you find yourself in front of a beautiful tree covered in tender pink or brilliant white blossom, a gracious adornment to the street. But as you look at it you realize that it is there according to some precise plan and not by chance. And the fact that it is not there by chance but according to a precise plan makes its beauty seem sad.

In Italy a tree in blossom at the roadside would be a delightful surprise. It would be there by chance, having sprung. out of the earth in sheer joy, and not because a calculated decision had been made that it should be there.

In London, which is a black and grey city, man has placed a few colours with precision and forethought. You can suddenly find a blue or red or pink front door among its black brothers. The buses that pass by in the grey air are painted a vivid red. These are colours that would be cheerful anywhere else, but here they are not cheerful; set in place in such an exact and deliberate way they are like the weak, sad smile of someone who doesn't know how to smile.

And the fire-engines, which do not have a strident siren but a sweetly ringing bell, are also red.

England is never vulgar. It is conventional, but not vulgar. Because it is sad it is never coarse. Vulgarity springs from coarseness and bullying. It also springs from fantasy and imagination.

Sometimes we think we notice vulgarity, in the strident voice or shrill laugh of a woman, in the violent colours of her make-up or in her straw-coloured hair. But we quickly realize that in this country vulgarity is always overpowered by melancholy.

The English have no imagination. They all dress in the same way. The women you see in the streets all have the same beige or transparent plastic raincoats which look like shower-curtains or tablecloths in restaurants. They all carry wicker shopping-baskets looped over one arm. The business men all wear the uniform we know — black bowler-hat, pinstripe trousers and umbrella. The artists who live in Chelsea and the students who dream about art and a dissipated, bohemian life have untidy red beards and check jackets with shapeless pockets. The girls of this type dress in skin-tight black trousers, high-necked sweaters and — in the rain — white shoes.

When they dress like this the young believe that they are proclaiming at the tops of their voices their unconventionality, originality, freedom, and the individual inspiration of their own thoughts. Yet it does not occur to them that the streets are full of thousands of young people exactly identical to themselves, with the same hairstyle, the same expression of naïve defiance, the same shoes.

The English have no imagination: and yet they do show imagination in two things — two only. In the evening-clothes worn by old ladies, and in their cafés.

In the evenings the ladies wear the most extraordinary clothes. And they lavishly paint their faces pink and yellow. They transform themselves from mousy little sparrows into peacocks and resplendent pheasants.

No one is surprised by them. But the English do not know what surprise is. No one ever turns his head to look at anyone else in the street.

England also expresses its sense of fantasy in its cafés and restaurants. They often give them foreign names to make them more attractive — 'Pustza', 'Chez Nous', 'Roma', 'Le Alpi'. When you look through the windows you see wispy climbing plants, Chinese lanterns, sharp peaks of rock, the blue of glaciers. Or you see skulls and cross-bones, black walls, black carpets, funereal candles — and because these places are often deserted a mournful silence reigns.

Because England is so dissatisfied with itself it tries to dress up in the borrowed feathers of a foreign glamour, or seeks out the *frisson* of funereal enticements.

However, the food and drink which you find in these Pustze, Alpi and sepulchres all has the same wretched taste. Imagination has not yet reached as far as the food and drink — it is still tangled up in the curtains, carpets and lanterns.

The English rarely show surprise. If it happens that someone faints in the street, everything is provided for. In a few seconds a chair is found for him, a glass of water, a uniformed nurse.

That people may faint in the street has been foreseen, and everything goes on around the patient automatically and promptly so that help is at hand.

But the English are profoundly astonished when we ask for a little water in a restaurant. They do not drink water, and always quench their thirst with endless cups of tea. They never taste wine or touch water. And so a request for a glass of water — that glass of water which arrives so promptly when someone faints in the street — disconcerts them. They bring it at last — a small glass containing a little tepid water, on a tray, with a teaspoon.

Perhaps they are right to camouflage their cafés and restaurants under foreign disguises, because when these places are unequivocally English such a squalid desperation reigns in them as to make anyone who enters think of suicide.

I have often wondered why there is such a feeling of desolation in English cafés. Perhaps it comes from their desolate social relationships. Every place where the English gather to chat to one another exudes melancholy. Indeed, nothing in the world is sadder than an English conversation, in which everyone is careful to keep to superficialities and never touch on anything essential. In order not to offend your neighbour, not to violate his privacy — which is sacred — an English conversation revolves around subjects that are extremely boring for everyone concerned, but in which there is no danger.

The English are a people completely without cynicism. Basically, beneath their guffaws of laughter which suddenly burst out and then seem to shatter dully without any echo, they are always serious. They still believe in certain values which have been forgotten everywhere else — in the seriousness of work, of study, of fidelity to oneself, to friends, to one's word.

Civilization, respect for one's fellow men, good government, the capacity to perceive and to provide for men's needs, help for the old and the sick — all this is certainly the fruit of an ancient and profound intelligence. But this intelligence is not at all visible or noticeable in the people you pass in the street. If you look round yourself you see no trace of it. If we pick someone out at random and talk to the first person who passes us in the street it is useless to expect words that indicate human intelligence.

When we go into a shop the assistant greets us with the words 'Can I help you?' But these are mere words. She immediately shows that she is quite incapable of helping us and is not at all interested in trying to. There is no flicker in her of any desire to come to an agreement with us or co-operate with us, of any wish to satisfy us. When she looks for what we want she does not extend her gaze two centimetres beyond the end of her nose.

English shop assistants are the stupidest shop assistants in the world.

But it is a stupidity in which there is no cynicism, insolence, bullying or contempt. It is a stupidity entirely lacking in vulgarity. It is never under any circumstances demeaning, and so it is not offensive. The assistants' eyes have the empty stunned stillness of the eyes of sheep on a limitless moor.

When we leave the shop the stunned empty eyes of the assistant follow us without having made any judgement about us or even considered us. They are eyes which forget us immediately, as soon as we have left their tiny field of vision.

And so if we happen to come across an assistant who is less stupid than the rest we feel ready to buy the whole shop out of sheer astonishment.

Italy is a country which is willing to submit itself to the worst governments. It is, as we know, a country ruled by disorder, cynicism, incompetence and confusion.

Nevertheless we are aware of intelligence circulating in the streets like a vivid bloodstream.

This is an intelligence which is clearly useless. It is not used to benefit any institution that might to some extent improve the human condition. All the same, it warms and consoles the heart, even if this is an illusory comfort and perhaps a foolish one.

In England intelligence is translated into deeds, but if we look for it among the people who pass us in the street we only find a faint glimmer and this — stupidly and unjustly certainly — gives us a feeling of loss and induces melancholy.

We are quickly infected by the English melancholy. It is a sheepish, stunned melancholy, a sort of empty bewilderment, and on its surface the conversations about the weather, the seasons — about all those things one can discuss without going too deeply into anything, without giving offence or being offended — linger like the constant quiet buzzing of mosquitoes.

However, the English seem to be somehow aware of their sadness and of the sadness which their country inspires in foreigners. When they are with foreigners they have an apologetic air and appear always anxious to get away. They live as if in eternal exile, dreaming of other skies.

I am always surprised that in Italy those who have adolescent children dream of nothing but sending them to England during the summer holidays. Particularly if they have children who, as often happens during adolescence, are going through a period of being shy, unsociable, sulky and sullen. Italian parents think of England as a cure for just such ailments. In fact, England has no effect at all. It is a country where people stay exactly as they are.

A timid person stays timid, an unsociable person stays unsociable. And over this initial timidity and unsociableness spreads the great, limitless English melancholy, like an endless moor in which the eyes can find no landmark.

Moreover, these parents vainly hope that their children will learn English during their summer visit — a language that is extremely difficult to learn, which very few foreigners know well, and which every Englishman speaks in his own way.

England is a country where people stay exactly as they are. The soul does not receive the slightest jolt. It stays always still, unchanging, protected by a gentle, temperate, humid climate without seasonal extremes, in the same way that the green of the fields (which it is impossible to imagine being greener) stays the same throughout the seasons, never eaten away by intense cold or devoured by the sun. The soul does not free itself from its vices but neither does it attach itself to new vices. Like the grass, the soul silently lulls itself in its green solitude, watered by the tepid rain.

There are very beautiful cathedrals. They are not hemmed in among houses and shops but set in the midst of green meadows. There are very beautiful cemeteries with simple tombstones here and there on the grass beside the cathedrals, where there is a profound peace. No walls enclose them; they exist in a perpetual intimacy with the life about them, but immersed in unsurpassable peace.

In the country of melancholy the mind always returns to death. It does not fear death because it sees the shadow of death as being like the vast shadow of the trees, and like the silence that is already present in the soul, lost in its green sleep.

# La Maison Volpé

Near my house in London there is a place called *La Maison Volpé*. What it is I do not know, as I have never been inside it: I think it is a restaurant or café. Perhaps I shall never go inside, and that name will keep its aura of mystery for me. But I have a feeling that when I remember London and the time I have spent here those syllables will echo in my ear, and all London will be summed up for me in that Parisian name.

From the outside nothing is visible except a door with glass windows covered by thick dull brown curtains made of tulle; the curtains are old, dusty and faded. Perhaps it is a restaurant, but when I go past it I am not aware of any smell — either good or bad; and I have never seen anyone pass through the door over which its strange name — *La Maison Volpé* — is spelt out in black and gilt lettering. Whether it is a café or a restaurant or a dance-hall, I have the feeling that any food or drink served in there must be ancient, moth-eaten and covered in dust like the curtains. It is on a more or less suburban street; between a garage and a shop that sells refrigerators the always hermetically sealed *Maison Volpé* sends out its nocturnal mystery, a promise of secret, exotic and possibly sinful pleasures implied by the black and gilt lettering of its name.

There are many places like *La Maison Volpé* in London; they appear in the most unexpected areas, they have extravagant names, and from the outside it is difficult to say what they are: they have a nocturnal, exotic, and vaguely sinful air to them and when you enter, during the day time, you find a mysterious twilight only slightly mitigated by the glow from a few little blue lamps: there are velvet carpets and walls painted black — but everything is made disappointingly ordinary by the sugar bowls on the tables, full of the brown cane sugar they use here. We quickly realize that absolutely nothing strange happens in these places, and the only thing to drink in them is weak tepid coffee eked out with milk. The people sitting at the tables have dressed with a certain care — you can see from their clothes that they have not dropped in by chance but that they have come intending to spend a few hours in this particular place, and, perhaps, to enjoy themselves. What enjoyment there might be in passing the time in a place so completely devoid of cheerfulness I do not know. You do not see lovers embracing one another, and the conversation is carried on in an educated undertone; the customers do not give the impression of being involved in the kind of intimate, passionate, lively conversations which occur between a man and a woman, or between friends, in our cafés. There is no kind of intimacy in that educated undertone. All the furnishings, the curtains, the carpets, the twilight atmosphere, seem to be there in order to suggest intimacy, but it remains an abstract proposition, a remote dream.

When Italians in London meet each other they talk about restaurants. In all London there is not one restaurant where it is pleasant to meet your friends, and chat and eat. The restaurants are either too crowded or too empty. And they are either stiff and priggish or squalid. Sometimes they manage to be equally both at once; sometimes the priggishness is more noticeable than the squalor — stiff chairs with high backs, ladies swathed in furs, silver decanters: sometimes it is the squalor which is the more noticeable and there is a kind of colourless neglect to the place; but wherever you are you eat more or less the same dishes, the same overdone steak with a little boiled tomato next to it, and a leaf of lettuce without either oil or salt.

There are restaurants that serve only roast chicken. Masses and masses of chickens turning on spits. The waiters dash from table to table carrying plates of chicken. No other kind of food is visible. We leave feeling so nauseated that it seems impossible — ever in our lives — to taste a piece of chicken again. There are also restaurants called 'The Egg and I'. In them there is nothing but eggs — stone cold, marmoreal, hard-boiled eggs over which a little dribble of mayonnaise has been squirted.

Restaurants and food are widely advertised in England. In the cinema, in the street, in the underground stations, in magazines you see huge, colourful pictures of food and drink. 'Oh, it is luxurious! It is delicious!'* At the cinema we see long advertisements for restaurants — Chinese, Indian, Spanish — with orchestras, palm trees, flowers, and customers who eat with a fez or a sombrero perched on their heads, who go into ecstasies in front of a plate on which we glimpse the usual overdone steak and solitary lettuce leaf. Images of ripening strawberries and endless pastures, which will become Kiaora ice-cream (which you can have 'here and now'*) or paper cups of Fresko milk ('Fresko is delicious! and full of vitamins'*) — follow each other on the screen. The city is full of invitations to eat and drink. On every corner you see a poster showing a boiled egg with the sensible suggestion 'Go to work on an egg'*. Or 'Drinka Pinta Milka Day'*. 'Babycham? I'd love a Babycham!'* Or, 'Have a chicken for your weekend'*.

But despite all this fuss which is made about food, for the English it remains simply 'food'*, which is a sad, generalized thing. In novels you read that 'some food'* was brought, no affectionate or specific description is given. The thousands of tins stacked up in the groceries carry pictures of the most various and mouthwatering

---

*An asterisk indicates phrases in English in the original.

animals — pheasants, partridges, different kinds of deer, and they are stamped with the enticing names of distant countries which it would be marvellous to visit. But anyone who has been here for some time is unimpressed, he knows very well that the contents of these tins are 'food'*, which is to say nothing. Nothing that could be eaten with enjoyment and a quiet mind anyway.

After you have lived here for a while you realize that you have to be careful when buying food. You cannot go into a cake-shop, choose a few cakes and then take them home and eat them. This simple, innocent act is out of the question here. Because those cakes — so prettily covered in chocolate and dotted with almonds — are, when you eat them, like a paste made of coal-dust or sand. I should, out of fairness, add that they are perfectly harmless. They are only horrible, innocuous but horrible, with the staleness of hundreds of years, but innocuous. The cakes placed next to the mummies in the tombs of the Pharaohs must have the same taste. And you cannot buy sweets with an easy mind either. They can be as hard as rocks; they can stick to the teeth and fill your mouth with a peculiar taste of salt.

A pall of sadness hangs over every place where food is sold or served. Even the windows of the green-grocers — full of beautiful-looking fruit, piles of grapefruit and bunches of bananas — these greengrocers' windows which are the same everywhere, in the stations of the underground, in the most distant suburbs and in the most remote rural villages, are always sad. Perhaps because they are so relentlessly identical to each other. Perhaps because we know that when this fruit is eaten it has no taste. But perhaps only because we are dealing with food, and that is something which is sad here.

Nevertheless the English are obsessed with the idea of food. Walking along the most remote country road, on the edge of a deep wood or of some desolate gorse-covered slope, we come across a little notice on which is written 'Teas, Luncheons, Snacks'*. We look around asking ourselves how, and by whom, such an enticing promise could be fulfilled. There is not a soul in sight. But yes, over there, a few steps further on, a caravan is waiting for us where we can actually have a cup of tea, or the usual sweet, tepid coffee, and ham sandwiches. Near the cash register there is also a large glass globe half full of bubbling orange juice on which — perhaps in order to convey a more intimate idea of freshness — someone has set one or two rubber oranges afloat.

Sometimes, instead of a caravan, we come across a little half-timbered house in the open countryside with the notice 'Farm'* on it, and the usual promise of 'Snacks'*. As we enter we imagine that we shall eat something local and unusual. The 'Farm'* is crowded with daytrippers from London who — at four in the' afternoon — are eating cod and chips. There is the usual globe of orange juice, and lined up next to the cash-register are the paper cups for Fresko ('Fresko is delicious!')* milk. The 'snacks'* are sandwiches. Those of the 'Farm'* are made with the usual pre-sliced flabby bread that is sold in Lyons and in every English grocer's shop. As far as the eye can see the countryside stretches — beautiful, green, rustling and damp, wild and at the same time gentle like no other in the world, silent, inedible and odourless. We are not aware of any smell of manure, animals, ploughed-up earth or straw, we do not hear the noises that we are used to hearing in the country — the creaking of carts or the trampling of hoofs. Clean, odourless cows are grazing in an enclosure. No one is looking after them; we see no herdsman, no dogs, no farm-workers. Sometimes it is possible to find a pub deep in the country; inside it is sumptuously decorated with red velvet and gilded cornices. It is identical to the pubs in central London, there is no difference. In one corner there is a little grate in which a fake coal fire or a fake log fire is burning; fake, but expertly done. The beer is drunk from big, heavy tankards of clouded glass. They bring the beer up from the cellars in barrels made of tin or zinc, and these inevitably make you think of sewage. But sometimes this happens in London too. Why don't they use a different kind of container? There is no why. The English are insensitive to certain mental associations. And perhaps those barrels are a sign of that deep distaste, that secret hatred which the English feel for food and drink. To me it seems that even some of the words they use to indicate food and drink have an unpleasant sound and reveal hatred and distaste: 'Snacks, Squash, Poultry'\*. Don't such words sound like insults?

Perhaps the English hatred for food is the sole cause of that obscure sadness which pervades every place where food is sold or served. If you disregard the showy fittings their cafés and restaurants are alarmingly like canteens for the poor. And on certain nights of every week in the doorways of even the most elegant restaurants in central London, in front of the most mysterious nightclubs with the strangest names, even in front of the mysterious *Maison Volpé*, you see huge, overflowing grey dustbins. Dustbins are not the prettiest things anywhere in the world. But I don't think that in any country in the world are they as large, grey, obvious and overflowing as they are here, giving off their grey stink and weighed down with desolate melancholy.

# He and I

He always feels hot, I always feel cold. In the summer when it really is hot he does nothing but complain about how hot he feels. He is irritated if he sees me put a jumper on in the evening.

He speaks several languages well; I do not speak any well. He manages — in his own way — to speak even the languages that he doesn't know.

He has an excellent sense of direction, I have none at all. After one day in a foreign city he can move about in it as thoughtlessly as a butterfly. I get lost in my own city; I have to ask directions so that I can get back home again. He hates asking directions; when we go by car to a town we don't know he doesn't want to ask directions and tells me to look at the map. I don't know how to read maps and I get confused by all the little red circles and he loses his temper.

He loves the theatre, painting, music, especially music. I do not understand music at all, painting doesn't mean much to me and I get bored at the theatre. I love and understand one thing in the world and that is poetry.

He loves museums, and I will go if I am forced to but with an unpleasant sense of effort and duty. He loves libraries and I hate them.

He loves travelling, unfamiliar foreign cities, restaurants. I would like to stay at home all the time and never move.

All the same I follow him on his many journeys. I follow him to museums, to churches, to the opera. I even follow him to concerts, where I fall asleep.

Because he knows the conductors and the singers, after the performance is over he likes to go and congratulate them. I follow him down long corridors lined with the singers' dressing-rooms and listen to him talking to people dressed as cardinals and kings.

He is not shy; I am shy. Occasionally however I have seen him be shy. With the police when they come over to the car armed with a notebook and pencil. Then he is shy, thinking he is in the wrong.

And even when he doesn't think he is in the wrong. I think he has a respect for established authority. I am afraid of established authority, but he isn't. He respects it. There is a difference. When I see a policeman coming to fine me I immediately think he is going to haul me off to prison. He doesn't think about prison; but, out of respect, he becomes shy and polite.

During the Montesi trial, because of his respect for established authority, we had very violent arguments.

He likes tagliatelle, lamb, cherries, red wine. I like minestrone, bread soup, omelettes, green vegetables.

He often says I don't understand anything about food, that I am like a great strong fat friar — one of those friars who devour soup made from greens in the darkness of their monasteries; but he, oh he is refined and has a sensitive palate. In restaurants he makes long inquiries about the wines; he has them bring two or three bottles then looks at them and considers the matter, and slowly strokes his beard.

There are certain restaurants in England where the waiter goes through a little ritual: he pours some wine into a glass so that the customer can test whether he likes it or not. He used to hate this ritual and always prevented the waiter from carrying it out by taking the bottle from him. I used to argue with him about this and say that you should let people carry out their prescribed tasks.

And in the same way he never lets the usherette at the cinema direct him to his seat. He immediately gives her a tip but dashes off to a completely different place from the one she shows him with her torch.

At the cinema he likes to sit very close to the screen. If we go with friends and they look for seats a long way from the screen, as most people do, he sits by himself in the front row. I can see well whether I am close to the screen or far away from it, but when we are with friends I stay with them out of politeness; all the same it upsets me because I could be next to him two inches from the screen, and when I don't sit next to him he gets annoyed with me.

We both love the cinema, and we are ready to see almost any kind of film at almost any time of day. But he knows the history of the cinema in great detail; he remembers old directors and actors who have disappeared and been forgotten long ago, and he is ready to travel miles into the most distant suburbs in search of some ancient silent film in which an actor appears — perhaps just for a few seconds — whom he affectionately associates with memories of his early childhood. I remember one Sunday afternoon in London; somewhere in the distant suburbs on the edge of the countryside they were showing a film from the 1930s, about the French Revolution, which he had seen as a child, and in which a famous actress of that time appeared for a moment or two. We set off by car in search of the street, which was a very long way off; it was raining, there was a fog, and we drove for hour after hour through identical suburbs, between rows of little grey houses, gutters and railings; I had the map on my knees and I couldn't read it and he lost his temper; at last, we found the cinema and sat in the completely deserted auditorium. But after a quarter of an hour, immediately after the brief appearance of the actress who was so important to him, he already wanted to go; I on the other hand, after seeing so many streets, wanted to see how the film finished. I don't remember whether we did what he wanted or what I wanted;

probably what he wanted, so that we left after a quarter of an hour, also because it was late — though we had set off early in the afternoon it was already time for dinner. But when I begged him to tell me how the film ended I didn't get a very satisfactory answer; because, he said, the story wasn't at all important, the only thing that mattered was those few moments, that actress's curls, gestures, profile.

I never remember actors' names, and as I am not good at remembering faces it is often difficult for me to recognize even the most famous of them. This infuriates him; his scorn increases as I ask him whether it was this one or that one; 'You don't mean to tell me,' he says, 'You don't mean to tell me that you didn't recognize William Holden!'

And in fact I didn't recognize William Holden. All the same, I love the cinema too; but although I have been seeing films for years I haven't been able to provide myself with any sort of cinematic education. But he has made an education of it for himself and he does this with whatever attracts his curiosity; I don't know how to make myself an education out of anything, even those things that I love best in life; they stay with me as scattered images, nourishing my life with memories and emotions but without filling the void, the desert of my education.

He tells me I have no curiosity, but this is not true. I am curious about a few, a very few, things. And when I have got to know them I retain scattered impressions of them, or the cadence of phrase, or a word. But my world, in which these completely unrelated (unless in some secret fashion unbeknown to me) impressions and cadences rise to the surface, is a sad, barren place. His world, on the other hand, is green and populous and richly cultivated; it is a fertile, well-watered countryside in which woods, meadows, orchards and villages flourish.

Everything I do is done laboriously, with great difficulty and uncertainty. I am very lazy, and if I want to finish anything it is absolutely essential that I spend hours stretched out on the sofa. He is never idle, and is always doing something; when he goes to lie down in the afternoons he takes proofs to correct or a book full of notes; he wants us to go to the cinema, then to a reception, then to the theatre — all on the same day. In one day he succeeds in doing, and in making me do, a mass of different things, and in meeting extremely diverse kinds of people. If I am alone and try to act as he does I get nothing at all done, because I get stuck all afternoon somewhere I had meant to stay for half an hour, or because I get lost and cannot find the right street, or because the most boring person and the one I least wanted to meet drags me off to the place I least wanted to go to.

If I tell him how my afternoon has turned out he says it is a completely wasted afternoon and is amused and makes fun of me and loses his temper; and he says that without him I am good for nothing.

I don't know how to manage my time; he does.

He likes receptions. He dresses casually, when everyone is dressed formally; the idea of changing his clothes in order to go to a reception never enters his head. He even goes in his old raincoat and crumpled hat; a woollen hat which he bought in London and which he wears pulled down over his eyes. He only stays for half an hour; he enjoys chatting with a glass in his hand for half an hour; he eats lots of *hors d'oeuvres*, and I eat almost none because when I see him eating so many I feel that I at least must be well-mannered and show some self-control and not eat too much; after half an hour, just as I am beginning to feel at ease and to enjoy myself, he gets impatient and drags me away.

I don't know how to dance and he does.

I don't know how to type and he does.

I don't know how to drive. If I suggest that I should get a licence too he disagrees. He says I would never manage it. I think he likes me to be dependant on him for some things.

I don't know how to sing and he does. He is a baritone. Perhaps he would have been a famous singer if he had studied singing.

Perhaps he would have been a conductor if he had studied music. When he listens to records he conducts the orchestra with a pencil. And he types and answers the telephone at the same time. He is a man who is able to do many things at once.

He is a professor and I think he is a good one.

He could have been many things. But he has no regrets about those professions he did not take up. I could only ever have followed one profession — the one I chose and which I have followed almost since childhood. And I don't have any regrets either about the professions I did not take up, but then I couldn't have succeeded at any of them.

I write stories, and for many years I have worked for a publishing house.

I don't work badly, or particularly well. All the same I am well aware of the fact that I would have been unable to work anywhere else. I get on well with my colleagues and my boss. I think that if I did not have the support of their friendship I would soon have become worn out and unable to work any longer.

For a long time I thought that one day I would be able to write screenplays for the cinema. But I never had the opportunity, or I did not know how to find it. Now I have lost all hope of writing screenplays. He wrote screenplays for a while, when he was younger. And he has worked in a publishing house. He has written stories. He has done all the things that I have done and many others too.

He is a good mimic, and does an old countess especially well. Perhaps he could also have been an actor.

Once, in London, he sang in a theatre. He was Job. He had to hire evening clothes; and there he was, in his evening clothes, in front of a kind of lectern; and he sang. He sang the words of Job; the piece called for something between speaking and singing. And I, in my box, was dying of fright. I was afraid he would get flustered, or that the trousers of his evening clothes would fall down.

He was surrounded by men in evening clothes and women in long dresses, who were the angels and devils and other characters in Job.

It was a great success, and they said that he was very good.

If I loved music I would love it passionately. But I don't understand it, and when he persuades me to go to concerts with him my mind wanders off and I think of my own affairs. Or I fall sound asleep.

I like to sing. I don't know how to sing and I sing completely out of tune; but I sing all the same — occasionally, very quietly, when I am alone. I know that I sing out of tune because others have told me so; my voice must be like the yowling of a cat. But I am not — in myself — aware of this, and singing gives me real pleasure. If he hears me he mimics me; he says that my singing is something quite separate from music, something invented by me.

When I was a child I used to yowl tunes I had made up. It was a long wailing kind of melody that brought tears to my eyes.

It doesn't matter to me that I don't understand painting or the figurative arts, but it hurts me that I don't love music, and I feel that my mind suffers from the absence of this love. But there is nothing I can do about it, I will never understand or love music. If I occasionally hear a piece of music that I like I don't know how to remember it; and how can I love something that I can't remember?

It is the words of a song that I remember. I can repeat words that I love over and over again. I repeat the tune that accompanies them too, in my own yowling fashion, and I experience a kind of happiness as I yowl.

When I am writing it seems to me that I follow a musical cadence or rhythm. Perhaps music was very close to my world, and my world could not, for whatever reason, make contact with it.

In our house there is music all day long. He keeps the radio on all day. Or plays records. Every now and again I protest a little and ask for a little silence in which to work; but he says that such beautiful music is certainly conducive to any kind of work.

He has bought an incredible number of records. He says that he owns one of the finest collections in the world.

In the morning when he is still in his dressing gown and dripping water from his bath, he turns the radio on, sits down at the typewriter and begins his strenuous, noisy, stormy day. He is superabundant in everything; he fills the bath to overflowing, and the same with the teapot and his cup of tea. He has an enormous number of shirts and ties. On the other hand he rarely buys shoes.

His mother says that as a child he was a model of order and precision; apparently once, on a rainy day, he was wearing white boots and white clothes and had to cross some muddy streams in the country — at the end of his walk he was immaculate and his clothes and boots had not one spot of mud on them. There is no trace in him of that former immaculate little boy. His clothes are always covered in stains. He has become extremely untidy.

But he scrupulously keeps all the gas bills. In drawers I find old gas bills, which he refuses to throw away, from houses we left long ago.

I also find old, shrivelled Tuscan cigars, and cigarette holders made from cherry wood.

I smoke a brand of king-size, filterless cigarettes called *Stop*, and he smokes his Tuscan cigars.

I am very untidy. But as I have got older I have come to miss tidiness, and I sometimes furiously tidy up all the cupboards. I think this is because I remember my mother's tidiness. I rearrange the linen and blanket cupboards and in the summer I reline every drawer with strips of white cloth. I rarely rearrange my papers because my mother didn't write and had no papers. My tidiness and untidiness are full of complicated feelings of regret and sadness. His untidiness is triumphant. He has decided that it is proper and legitimate for a studious person like himself to have an untidy desk.

He does not help me get over my indecisiveness, or the way I hesitate before doing anything, or my sense of guilt. He tends to make fun of every tiny thing I do. If I go shopping in the market he follows me and spies on me. He makes fun of the way I shop, of the way I weigh the oranges in my hand unerringly choosing, he says, the worst in the whole market; he ridicules me for spending an hour over the shopping, buying onions at one stall, celery at another and fruit at another. Sometimes he does the shopping to show me how quickly he can do it; he unhesitatingly buys everything from one stall and then manages to get the basket delivered to the house. He doesn't buy celery because he cannot abide it.

And so — more than ever — I feel I do everything inadequately or mistakenly. But if I once find out that he has made a mistake I tell him so over and over again until he is exasperated. I can be very annoying at times.

His rages are unpredictable, and bubble over like the head on beer. My rages are unpredictable too, but his quickly disappear whereas mine leave a noisy nagging trail behind them which must be very annoying — like the complaining yowl of a cat.

Sometimes in the midst of his rage I start to cry, and instead of quietening him down and making him feel sorry for me this infuriates him all the more. He says my tears are just play-acting, and perhaps he is right. Because in the middle of my tears and his rage I am completely calm.

I never cry when I am really unhappy.

There was a time when I used to hurl plates and crockery on the floor during my rages. But not any more. Perhaps because I am older and my rages are less violent, and also because I dare not lay a finger on our plates now; we bought them one day in London, in the Portobello Road, and I am very fond of them.

The price of those plates, and of many other things we have bought, immediately underwent a substantial reduction in his memory. He likes to think he did not spend very much and that he got a bargain. I know the price of that dinner service — it was £16, but he says £12. And it is the same with the picture of King Lear that is in our dining room, and which he also bought in the Portobello Road (and then cleaned with onions and potatoes); now he says he paid a certain sum for it, but I remember that it was much more than that.

Some years ago he bought twelve bedside mats in a department store. He bought them because they were cheap, and he thought he ought to buy them; and he bought them as an argument against me because he considered me to be incapable of buying things for the house. They were made of mud-coloured matting and they quickly became very unattractive; they took on a corpse-like rigidity and were hung from a wire line on the kitchen balcony, and I hated them. I used to remind him of them, as an example of bad shopping; but he would say that they had cost very little indeed, almost nothing. It was a long time before I could bring myself to throw them out — because there were so many of them, and because just as I was about to get rid of them it occurred to me that I could use them for rags. He and I both find throwing things away difficult; it must be a kind of Jewish caution in me, and the result of my extreme indecisiveness; in him it must be a defence against his impulsiveness and open-handedness.

He buys enormous quantities of bicarbonate of soda and aspirins.

Now and again he is ill with some mysterious ailment of his own; he can't explain what he feels and stays in bed for a day completely wrapped up in the sheets; nothing is visible except his beard and the tip of his red nose. Then he takes bicarbonate of soda and aspirins in doses suitable for a horse, and says that I cannot understand because I am always well, I am like those great fat strong friars who go out in the wind and in all weathers and come to no harm; he on the other hand is sensitive and delicate and suffers from mysterious ailments. Then in the evening he is better and goes into the kitchen and cooks himself tagliatelle.

When he was a young man he was slim, handsome and finely built; he did not have a beard but long, soft moustaches instead, and he looked like the actor Robert Donat. He was like that about twenty years ago when I first knew him, and I remember that he used to wear an elegant kind of Scottish flannel shirt. I remember that one evening he walked me back to the *pensione* where I was living; we walked together along the *Via Nazionale*. I already felt that I was very old and had been through a great deal and had made many mistakes, and he seemed a boy to me, light years away from me. I don't remember what we talked about on that evening walking along the *Via Nazionale*; nothing important, I suppose, and the idea that we would become husband and wife was light years away from me. Then we lost sight of each other, and when we met again he no longer looked like Robert Donat, but more like Balzac. When we met again he still wore his Scottish shirts but on him now they looked like garments for a polar expedition; now he had his beard and on his head he wore his ridiculous crumpled woollen hat; everything about him put you in mind of an imminent departure for the North Pole. Because, although he always feels hot, he has the habit of dressing as if he were surrounded by snow, ice and polar bears; or he dresses like a Brazilian coffee-planter, but he always dresses differently from everyone else.

If I remind him of that walk along the *Via Nazionale* he says he remembers it, but I know he is lying and that he remembers nothing; and I sometimes ask myself if it was us, these two people, almost twenty years ago on the *Via Nazionale*; two people who conversed so politely, so urbanely, as the sun was setting; who chatted a little about everything perhaps and about nothing; two friends talking, two young intellectuals out for a walk; so young, so educated, so uninvolved, so ready to judge one another with kind impartiality; so ready to say goodbye to one another for ever, as the sun set, at the corner of the street.

# Part Two

# The Son of Man

There has been a war and people have seen so many houses reduced to rubble that they no longer feel safe in their own homes which once seemed so quiet and secure. This is something that is incurable and will never be cured no matter how many years go by. True, we have a lamp on the table again, and a little vase of flowers, and pictures of our loved ones, but we can no longer trust any of these things because once, suddenly, we had to leave them behind, or because we have searched through the rubble for them in vain.

It is useless to believe that we could recover from twenty years like those we have been through. Those of us who have been fugitives will never be at peace. A ring at the door-bell in the middle of the night can only mean the word 'police' to us. And it is useless for us to tell ourselves over and over again that behind the word 'police' there are now friendly faces from whom we can ask for help and protection. This word always fills us with fear and suspicion. When I look at my sleeping children I think with relief that I will not have to wake them and run off into the night. But it is not a deep, lasting relief. It always seems to me that some day or other we shall once again have to get up and run off in the middle of the night, and leave everything — the quiet rooms, our letters, mementoes, clothes — behind us.

Once the experience of evil has been endured it is never forgotten. Someone who has seen a house collapse knows only too clearly what frail things little vases of flowers and pictures and white walls are. He knows only too well what a house is made of. A house is made of bricks and mortar and can collapse. A house is not particularly solid. It can collapse from one moment to the next. Behind the peaceful little vases of flowers, behind the teapots and carpets and waxed floors there is the other true face of a house — the hideous face of a house that has been reduced to rubble.

We shall not get over this war. It is useless to try. We shall never be people who go peacefully about their business, who think and study and manage their lives quietly. Something has happened to our houses. Something has happened to us. We shall never be at peace again.

We have seen reality's darkest face, and it no longer horrifies us. And there are still those who complain that writers use bitter, violent language, that they write about cruel, distressing things, that they present reality in the worst possible light.

We cannot lie in our books and we cannot lie in any of the things we do. And perhaps this is the one good thing that has come out of the war. Not to lie, and not to allow others to lie to us. Such is the nature of the young now, of our generation. Those who are older than us are still too fond of falsehoods, of the veils and masks with which they hide reality. Our language saddens and offends them. They do not understand our attitude to reality. We are close to the truth of things. This is the only good the war has given us, but it has given it only to the young. It has given nothing but fear and a sense of insecurity to the old. And we who are young are also afraid, we also feel insecure in our homes, but we are not made defenceless by this fear. We have a toughness and strength which those who are older than us have never known.

For some the war started only with the war, with houses reduced to rubble and with the Germans, but for others it started as long ago as the first years of Fascism, and consequently for them the feeling of insecurity and constant danger is far greater. Danger, the feeling that you must hide, the feeling that — without warning — you will have to leave the warmth of your bed and your house, for many of us all this started many years ago. It crept into our childish games, followed us to our desks at school and taught us to see enemies everywhere. This is how it was for many of us in Italy, and elsewhere, and we believed that one day we would be able to walk without anxiety down the streets of our own cities, but now that we can perhaps walk there without anxiety we realize that we shall never be cured of this sickness. And so we are constantly forced to seek out a new strength, a new toughness with which to face whatever reality may confront us. We have been driven to look for an inward peace which is not the product of carpets and little vases of flowers.

There is no peace for the son of man. The foxes and the wolves have their holes, but the son of man hath not where to lay his head. Our generation is a generation of men. It is not a generation of foxes and wolves. Each of us would dearly like to rest his head somewhere, to have a little warm, dry nest. But there is no peace for the son of man. Each of us at some time in his life has had the illusion that he could sleep somewhere safely, that he could take possession of some certainty, some faith, and there rest his limbs. But all the certainties of the past have been snatched away from us, and faith has never after all been a place for sleeping in.

And we are a people without tears. The things that moved our parents do not move us at all. Our parents and those older than us disapprove of the way we bring up our children. They would like us to lie to our children as they lied to us. They would like our children to play with woolly toys in pretty pink rooms with little trees and rabbits painted on the walls. They would like us to surround their infancy with veils and lies, and carefully hide the truth of things from them. But we cannot do this. We cannot do this to children whom we have woken in the middle of the night and tremblingly dressed in the darkness so that we could flee with them or hide them, or simply because the air-raid sirens were lacerating the skies. We cannot do this to children who have seen terror and horror in our faces. We cannot bring ourselves to tell these children that we found them under cabbages, or that when a person dies he goes on a long journey.

There is an unbridgeable abyss between us and the previous generation. The dangers they lived through were trivial and their houses were rarely reduced to rubble. Earthquakes and fires were not phenomena that happened constantly and to everyone. The women did their knitting and told the cook what to make for lunch and invited their friends to houses that did not collapse. Everyone thought and studied and managed his life quietly. It was a different time and probably very fine in its way. But we are tied to our suffering, and at heart we are glad of our destiny as men.

# My Vocation

My vocation is to write and I have known this for a long time. I hope I won't be misunderstood; I know nothing about the value of the things I am able to write. I know that writing is my vocation. When I sit down to write I feel extraordinarily at ease, and I move in an element which, it seems to me, I know extraordinarily well; I use tools that are familiar to me and they fit snugly in my hands. If I do something else, if I study a foreign language or try to learn history or geography or shorthand or if I try and speak in public or take up knitting or go on a journey, I suffer and constantly ask myself how others do these things: it always seems to me that there must be some correct way of doing these things which others know about and I don't. And it seems to me that I am deaf and blind and I feel a sort of sickness in the pit of my stomach. But when I write I never imagine that there is perhaps a better way of writing which other writers follow. I am not interested in what other writers do. But here I had better make it plain that I can only write stories. If I try to write a critical essay or an article that has been commissioned for a newspaper I don't do it very well. I have to search laboriously, as it were outside myself, for what I am writing now. I can do it a little better than I can learn a foreign language or speak in public, but only a little better. And I always feel that I am cheating the reader with words that I have borrowed or filched from various places. I suffer and feel that I am in exile. But when I write stories I am like someone who is in her own country, walking along streets that she has known since

she was a child, between walls and trees that are hers. My
vocation is to write stories — invented things or things
which I can remember from my own life, but in any case
stories, things that are concerned only with memory and
imagination and have nothing to do with erudition. This
is my vocation and I shall work at it till I die. I am very
happy with my vocation and I would not change it for
anything in the world. I realized that it was my vocation
a long time ago. Between the ages of five and ten I was
still unsure, and sometimes I imagined that I would be a
painter, sometimes that I would ride out on horseback
and conquer countries, sometimes that I would invent
new machines that would be very important. But I have
known since I was ten, and I worked as hard as I could at
poems and novels. I still have those poems. The first
poems are clumsy and they have errors of versification in
them, but they are quite pleasant; and then, little by little,
as time passed I wrote poems that became less and less
clumsy but more and more boring and silly. However I
didn't know this and I was ashamed of the clumsy
poems, while those that were silly and not so clumsy
seemed to me to be very beautiful, and I used to think
that one day some famous poet would discover them and
have them published and write long articles about me; I
imagined the words and phrases of those articles and I
composed them, from beginning to end, in my head. I
imagined that I would win the Fracchia prize. I had heard
that there was such a prize for writers. As I was unable to
publish my poems in a book, since I didn't know any
famous poets, I copied them neatly into an exercise book
and drew a little flower on the title page and made an
index and everything. It became very easy for me to
write poems. I wrote about one a day. I realized that if I
didn't want to write it was enough for me to read some
poems by Pascoli or Gozzano or Corazzini and then I
immediately wanted to. My poems came out as imitation
Pascoli or imitation Gozzano or imitation Corazzini and

then finally very imitation D'Annunzio when I found out that he also existed. However I never thought that I would write poetry all my life. I wanted to write novels sooner or later. I wrote three or four during those years. There was one called *Marion or the Gipsy Girl*, another called *Molly and Dolly* (a humorous detective story) and another called *A Woman* (*à la* D'Annunzio; in the second person; the story of a woman abandoned by her husband; I remember that there was also a cook who was a negress) and then one that was very long and complicated with terrible stories of kidnapped girls and carriages so that I was too afraid to write it when I was alone in the house: I can remember nothing about it except that there was one phrase which pleased me very much and that tears came into my eyes as I wrote it, 'He said: ah! Isabella is leaving'. The chapter finished with this phrase which was very important because it was said by the man who loved Isabella although he did not know this as he had not yet confessed it to himself. I don't remember anything about this man (I think he had a reddish beard), Isabella had long black hair with blue highlights in it, I don't know anything else about her; I know that for a long time I would feel a shiver of joy whenever I said 'Ah! Isabella is leaving' to myself. I also often used to repeat a phrase which I had found in a serialized novel in *Stampa* which went like this, 'Murderer of Gilonne, where have you put my child?' But I was not as sure about my novels as I was about the poems. When I reread them I always discovered a weakness somewhere or other, something wrong which spoiled everything and which was impossible to change. I always used to muddle up the past and the present, I was unable to fix the story in a particular time; parts of it were convents and carriages and a general feeling of the French Revolution, and parts of it were policemen with truncheons; and then all of a sudden there would be a little grey housewife with a sewing-machine and cats as in Carola Prosperi's novels, and this didn't go very well with the carriages and convents. I wavered between Carola Prosperi and Victor Hugo and Nick Carter's stories; I didn't really know what I wanted to do. I was also very keen on Annie Vivanti. There is a phrase in *The Devourers* when she is writing to a stranger and says to him, 'I dress in brown'. This was another phrase which, for a long time, I repeated to myself. During the day I used to murmur to myself these phrases which gave me so much pleasure: 'Murderer of Gilonne', 'Isabella is leaving', 'I dress in brown', and I felt immensely happy.

Writing poetry was easy. I was very pleased with my poems, to me they seemed almost perfect. I could not see what difference there was between them and real, published poems by real poets. I could not see why when I gave them to my brothers to read they laughed and said I would have done better to study Greek. I thought that perhaps my brothers didn't know much about poetry. Meanwhile I had to go to school and study Greek, Latin, mathematics, history — and I suffered a good deal and felt I was in exile. I spent my days in writing poems and copying them out in exercise books; I did not study for my lessons so I used to set the alarm for five in the morning. The alarm went off but I went on sleeping. I woke at seven, when there was no longer any time to study and I had to dress to go to school. I was not happy, I was always extremely afraid and filled with feelings of guilt and confusion. When I got to school I studied history during the Latin lesson, Greek during the history lesson, and so on, and I learnt nothing. For quite a while I thought it was all worth it because my poems were so beautiful, but at a certain moment I began to think that perhaps they were not so beautiful and it became tedious for me to write them and take the trouble to find subjects; it seemed to me that I had already dealt with every possible subject, and used all the possible words and rhymes — *speranza, lontananza; pensiero, mistero; vento, argento*; *fragranza*, *speranza* (hope, distance; thought, mystery; wind, silver; fragrance, hope). I couldn't find anything else to say. Then a very nasty period began for me, and I spent the afternoons playing about with words that no longer gave me any pleasure while at the same time I felt guilty and ashamed about school. It never entered my head that I had mistaken my vocation — I wanted to write as much as ever, it was just that I could not understand why my days had suddenly become so barren and empty of words.

The first serious piece I wrote was a story. A short story of five or six pages; it came from me like a miracle in a single evening, and when afterwards I went to bed I was tired, bewildered, worn out. I had the feeling that it was a serious piece, the first that I had ever written: the poems and the novels about girls and carriages suddenly seemed very far away from me, they were the naïve and ridiculous creatures of another age and they belonged to a time that had disappeared for good. There were characters in this new story. Isabella and the man with the reddish beard were not characters; I didn't know anything about them beyond the words and phrases with which I described them — they appeared as if at random and not by my design. I had chosen the words and phrases I used for them by chance; it was as if I had a sack and had indiscriminately pulled out of it now a beard and now a cook who was a negress or some other usable item. But this time it was not a game. This time I had invented characters with names that I could not possibly have changed; I could not have changed any part of them and I knew a great deal about them — I knew how their lives had been up to the day of my story even though I did not talk about this in the story as it was not necessary. And I knew all about the house, the bridge, the moon and the river. I was seventeen and I had failed in Latin, Greek and mathematics. I had cried a lot when I found out. But now that I had written the story I felt a little less ashamed. It was summer, a summer night. A window that gave on to the garden was open and dark moths fluttered about the lamp. I had written my story on squared paper and I had felt happy as never before in my life; I felt I had a wealth of thoughts and words within me. The man was called Maurizio, the woman was called Anna and the child was called Villi, and the bridge, the moon and the river were also there. These things existed in me. And the man and the woman were neither good nor evil, but funny and a little sad and it seemed to me that I had discovered how people in books should be — funny and at the same time sad. Whichever way I looked at this story it seemed beautiful to me: there were no mistakes in it; everything happened as it should, at the right time. At that moment it seemed to me that I could write millions of stories.

And in fact I wrote quite a few, at intervals of a month or two — some were quite good and some not so good. Now I discovered that it is tiring to write something seriously. It is a bad sign if it doesn't make you tired. You cannot hope to write something serious frivolously flitting hither and thither, as it were with one hand tied behind your back. You cannot get off so lightly. When someone writes something seriously he is lost in it, he is sucked down into it up to his eyebrows; and if there is a very strong emotion that is preoccupying him, if he is very happy or very unhappy for some let us say mundane reason which has nothing to do with the piece he is writing, then if what he is writing is real and deserves to live all those other feelings will become dormant in him. He cannot hope to keep his dear happiness or dear unhappiness whole and fresh before him; everything goes off into the distance and vanishes and he is left alone with his page; no happiness or unhappiness that is not strictly relevant to that page can exist in him, he cannot possess or belong to anything else — and if it does not happen like this, well that is a sign that the page is worthless.

And so for a certain period — which lasted about six years — I wrote short stories. Since I had discovered that characters existed it seemed to me that to *have* a character was enough to make a story. So I was always hunting for characters, I looked at the people in the tram and on the street and when I found a face that seemed suitable for a story I wove some moral details and a little anecdote around it. I also went hunting for details of dress and people's appearance, and how their houses looked inside; if I went into a new room I tried to describe it silently to myself, and I tried to find some small detail which would fit well in a story. I kept a notebook in which I wrote down some of the details I had discovered, or little similes, or episodes which I promised myself I would use in stories. For example I would write in my notebook 'She came out of the bathroom trailing the cord of her dressing-gown behind her like a long tail', 'How the lavatory stinks in this house — the child said to him — When I go, I hold my breath — he added sadly', 'His curls like bunches of grapes', 'Red and black blankets on an unmade bed', 'A pale face like a peeled potato'. But I discovered how difficult it was to use these phrases when I was writing a story. The notebook became a kind of museum of phrases that were crystallized and embalmed and very difficult to use. I tried endlessly to slip the red and black blankets or the curls like bunches of grapes into a story but I never managed to. So the notebook was no help to me. I realized that in this vocation there is no such thing as 'savings'. If someone thinks 'that's a fine detail and I don't want to waste it in the story I'm writing at the moment, I've plenty of good material here, I'll keep it in reserve for another story I'm going to write', that detail will crystallize inside him and he won't be able to use it. When someone writes a story he should throw the best of everything into it, the best of whatever he possesses and has seen, all the best things that he has accumulated throughout his life. If you carry details around inside yourself for a long time without making use of them, they wear out and waste away. Not only details but everything, all your ideas and clever notions. At the time when I was writing short stories made up of characters I had chanced on, and minute descriptive details, at that time I once saw a hand-cart being pushed through the street and on it was a huge mirror in a gilded frame. The greenish evening sky was reflected in it and as I stopped to watch while it went past I was feeling extremely happy, and I had the impression that something important had happened. I had been feeling very happy even before I saw the mirror, and it suddenly seemed to me that in the greenish resplendent mirror with its gilded frame the image of my own happiness was passing by me. For a long time I thought that I would put this in a story, for a long time simply remembering that hand-cart with the mirror on top of it made me want to write. But I was never able to include it anywhere and finally I realised that the image had died in me. Nevertheless it was very important. Because at the time when I was writing my short stories I always concentrated on grey, squalid people and things, I sought out a contemptible kind of reality lacking in glory. There was a certain malignancy in the taste I had at that time for finding minute details, an avid, mean desire for little things — little as fleas are little; I was engaged on an obstinate, scandal-mongering hunt for fleas. The mirror on the hand-cart seemed to offer me new possibilities, perhaps the ability to look at a more glorious and splendid kind of reality which did not require minute descriptions and cleverly noticed details but which could be conveyed in one resplendent, felicitous image.

In the last analysis I despised the characters in the short stories I was writing at that time. Since I had discovered that it works well if a character is sad and comic I made characters who, because of their comic and pitiable qualities, were so contemptible and lacking in glory that I myself could not love them. My characters always had some nervous tic or obsession or physical deformity, or some rather ridiculous bad habit — they had a broken arm in a black sling, or they had sties in their eyes, or they stuttered, or they scratched their buttocks as they talked, or they limped a little. I always had to characterize them in some such way. For me this was a method of running away from my fear that they would turn out too vague, a way of capturing their humanity (which, subconsciously, I did not believe in). Because at that time I did not realize — though when I saw the mirror on the hand-cart I began, confusedly, to realize it — that I was no longer dealing with characters but with puppets, quite well painted and resembling men, but puppets. When I invented them I immediately characterized them, I marked them with some grotesque detail, and there was something nasty in this; I had a kind of malign resentment against reality. It was not a resentment based on anything real, because at that time I was a happy girl, but it appeared as a kind of reaction against naïvety; it was that special resentment with which a naïve person who always thinks she is being made a fool of defends herself — the resentment of a peasant who finds himself in a city for a while and sees thieves everywhere. At first I was bold, because this seemed to me to be a great ironic triumph over the naïvely pathetic effusions which were all too apparent in my poems. Irony and nastiness seemed to be very important weapons in my hands; I thought they would help me write like a man, because at that time I wanted terribly to write like a man and I had a horror of anyone realizing from what I wrote that I was a woman. I almost always invented male characters because they would be the furthest and most separate from myself.

I became reasonably good at blocking out a story, at getting rid of superfluous material and introducing details and conversations at the appropriate moments. wrote dry, clear stories that contained no blunders or

mistakes of tone and that came to a convincing conclusion. But after a while I had had enough of this. The
faces of people in the street no longer said anything
interesting to me. Someone had a sty and someone had
his cap on back to front and someone was wearing a scarf
instead of a shirt, but these things no longer mattered to
me. I was fed up with looking at things and people and
describing them to myself. The world became silent for
me. I could no longer find words to describe it, I no
longer had any words capable of giving me pleasure. I
didn't have anything anymore. I tried to remember the
mirror, but even that had died in me. I carried a burden
of embalmed objects around inside of me — silent faces
and ashen words, places and voices and gestures that
were a dead weight on my heart, that had no flicker of
life in them. And then my children were born and when
they were very little I could not understand how anyone
could sit herself down to write if she had children. I did
not see how I could separate myself from them in order
to follow someone or other's fortunes in a story. I began
to feel contempt for my vocation. Now and again I
longed for it desperately and felt that I was in exile, but I
tried to despise it and make fun of it and occupy myself
solely with the children. I believed I had to do this. I
spent my time on creamed rice and creamed barley and
wondering whether there was sun or not or wind or not
so that I could take the children out for a walk. The
children seemed extremely important to me because they
were a way of leaving my stupid stories and stupid
embalmed characters behind. But I felt a ferocious
longing within me and sometimes at night I almost wept
when I remembered how beautiful my vocation was. I
thought that I would recover it some day or other but I
did not know when: I thought that I would have to wait
till my children grew up and left me. Because the feeling I
then had for my children was one that I had not yet learnt
to control. But then little by little I learnt, and it did not

even take that long. I still made tomato sauce and
semolina, but simultaneously I thought about what I
could be writing. At that time we were living in very
beautiful countryside, in the south. I remembered my
own city's streets and hills, and those streets and hills
mingled with the streets and hills and meadows of the
place where we were, and a new nature, something that I
was once again able to love, appeared. I felt homesick for
my city and in retrospect I loved it very much, I loved
and understood it in a way that I had never done when I
lived there, and I also loved the place where we were then
living — a countryside that was white and dusty in the
southern sunlight; wide meadows of scorched, bristling
grass stretched away from my windows, and a memory
of the avenues and plane-trees and high houses of my city
assailed me; all this slowly took fire in me and I had a
very strong desire to write. I wrote a long story, the
longest I had ever written. I started writing again like
someone who has never written, because it was a long
time since I had written anything, and the words seemed
rinsed and fresh, everything was new and as it were
untouched, and full of taste and fragrance. I wrote in the
afternoons while a local girl took my children out for a
walk, and I wrote greedily and joyfully; it was a beautiful
autumn and I felt very happy every day. I put a few
invented people into my story and a few real people from
the countryside where we were living; and some of the
words that came to me as I was writing were idioms and
imprecations local to that area, and which I had not
known before, and these new expressions were like a
yeast that fermented and gave life to all the old words.
The main character was a woman, but very different
from myself. Now I no longer wanted to write like a
man, because I had had children and I thought I knew a
great many things about tomato sauce and even if I didn't
put them into my story it helped my vocation that I knew
them; in a strange, remote way these things also helped

my vocation. It seemed to me that women knew things about their children that a man could never know. I wrote my story very quickly, as if I were afraid that it would run away. I called it a novel, but perhaps it was not a novel. But up till then I had always written very quickly, and always very short things, and at a certain moment I thought I realized why. Because I had brothers who were much older than me and when I was small if I talked at table they always told me to be quiet. And so I was used to speaking very fast, in a headlong fashion with the smallest possible number of words, and always afraid that the others would start talking among themselves again and stop listening to me. Perhaps this seems a rather stupid explanation; nevertheless that is how it was.

I said that the time when I was writing what I called a novel was a very happy time for me. Nothing serious had ever happened in my life, I knew nothing about sickness or betrayal or loneliness or death. Nothing in my life had ever fallen to pieces, except futile things, nothing dear to my heart had ever been snatched away from me. I had only suffered from the listless melancholy of adolescence and the pain of not knowing how to write. And so I was happy in a fulfilled, calm way, without fear or anxiety, and with a complete faith in the stability and durability of earthly happiness. When we are happy we feel that we are cooler, clearer, more separate from reality. When we are happy we tend to create characters who are very different from ourselves; we see them in a cold, clear light as things separate from us. While our imagination and inventive energy work assertively within us we avert our eyes from our own happy, contented state and pitilessly — with a free, cruel, ironic, proud gaze — fix them on other beings. It is easy for us to invent characters, many characters, who are fundamentally different from us, and it is easy for us to construct our stories solidly — they are as it were well-drained and stand in a cold, clear light.

What we then lack, when we are happy in this special way that has no tears or anxiety or fear in it, what we then lack is any tender, intimate sympathy with our characters and with the places and things we write about. What we lack is compassion. Superficially we are much more generous in the sense that we always find the strength to be interested in others and devote our time to them — we are not that preoccupied with ourselves because we don't need anything. But this interest of ours in others, which is so lacking in tenderness, can only get at a few relatively external aspects of their characters. The world has only one dimension for us and lacks secrets and shadows; we are able to guess at and create the sadness we have not experienced by virtue of the imaginative strength within us, but we always see it in a sterile, frozen light as something that does not concern us and that has no roots within us.

Our personal happiness or unhappiness, our *terrestrial* condition, has a great importance for the things we write. I said before that at the moment someone is writing he is miraculously driven to forget the immediate circumstances of his own life. This is certainly true. But whether we are happy or unhappy leads us to write in one way or another. When we are happy our imagination is stronger; when we are unhappy our memory works with greater vitality. Suffering makes the imagination weak and lazy; it moves, but unwillingly and heavily, with the weak movements of someone who is ill, with the weariness and caution of sick, feverish limbs; it is difficult for us to turn our eyes away from our own life and our own state, from the thirst and restlessness that pervade us. And so memories of our own past constantly crop up in the things we write, our own voice constantly echoes there and we are unable to silence it. A particular sympathy grows up between us and the characters that we invent — that our debilitated imagination is still just able to invent — a sympathy that is tender and almost maternal, warm and damp with tears, intimately physical and stifling. We are deeply, painfully rooted in every being and thing in the world, the world which has become filled with echoes and trembling and shadows, to which we are bound by a devout and passionate pity. Then we risk foundering on a dark lake of stagnant, dead water, and dragging our mind's creations down with us, so that they are left to perish among dead rats and rotting flowers in a dark, warm whirlpool. As far as the things we write are concerned there is a danger in grief just as there is a danger in happiness. Because poetic beauty is a mixture of ruthlessness, pride, irony, physical tenderness, of imagination and memory, of clarity and obscurity — and if we cannot gather all these things together we are left with something meagre, unreliable and hardly alive.

And you have to realize that you cannot hope to console yourself for your grief by writing. You cannot deceive yourself by hoping for caresses and lullabies from your vocation. In my life there have been interminable, desolate empty Sundays in which I desperately wanted to write something that would console me for my loneliness and boredom, so that I could be calmed and soothed by phrases and words. But I could not write a single line. My vocation has always rejected me, it does not want to know about me. Because this vocation is never a consolation or a way of passing the time. It is not a companion. This vocation is a master who is able to beat us till the blood flows, a master who reviles and condemns us. We must swallow our saliva and our tears and grit our teeth and dry the blood from our wounds and serve him. Serve him when he asks. Then he will help us up on to our feet, fix our feet firmly on the ground; he will help us overcome madness and delirium, fever and despair. But he has to be the one who gives the orders and he always refuses to pay attention to us when we need him.

After the time when I lived in the South I got to know grief very well — a real, irremediable and incurable grief that shattered my life, and when I tried to put it together again I realized that I and my life had become something irreconcilable with what had gone before. Only my vocation remained unchanged, but it is profoundly misleading to say that even that was unchanged — the tools were still the same but the way I used them had altered. At first I hated it, it disgusted me, but I knew very well that I would end up returning to it, and that it would save me. Sometimes I would think that I had not been so unfortunate in my life and that I was unjust when I accused destiny of never having shown me any kindness, because it had given me my three children and my vocation. Besides, I could not imagine my life without my vocation. It was always there, it had never left me for a moment, and when I believed that it slept its vigilant, shining eyes were still watching me.

Such is my vocation. It does not produce much money and it is always necessary to follow some other vocation simultaneously in order to live. Though sometimes it produces a little, and it is very satisfying to have money because of it — it is like receiving money and presents from the hands of someone you love. Such is my vocation. I do not, I repeat, know much about the value of the results it has given me or could give me: or it would be better to say that I know the relative though certainly not the absolute value of the results I have already obtained. When I write something I usually think it is very important and that I am a very fine writer. I think this happens to everyone. But there is one corner of my mind in which I know very well what I am, which is a small, a very small writer. I swear I know it. But that doesn't matter much to me. Only, I don't want to think about names: I can see that if I am asked 'a small writer like who?' it would sadden me to think of the names of other small writers. I prefer to think that no one has ever been like me, however small, however much a mosquito or a flea of a writer I may be. The important thing is to be convinced that this really is your vocation, your profession, something you will do all your life. But as a vocation it is no joke. There are innumerable dangers besides those I have mentioned. We are constantly threatened with grave dangers whenever we write a page. There is the danger of suddenly starting to be flirtatious and of singing. I always have a crazy desire to sing and I have to be very careful that I don't. And there is the danger of cheating with words that do not really exist within us, that we have picked up by chance from outside of ourselves and which we skilfully slip in because we have become a bit dishonest. There is the danger of cheating and being dishonest. As you see, it is quite a difficult vocation, but it is the finest one in the world. The days and houses of our life, the days and houses of the people with whom we are involved, books and images and thoughts and conversations — all these things feed it, and it grows within us. It is a vocation which also feeds on terrible things, it swallows the best and the worst in our lives and our evil feelings flow in its blood just as much as our benevolent feelings. It feeds itself, and grows within us.

# Silence

I heard *Pelléas et Mélisande*. I know nothing about music, but I found myself comparing words from old opera libretti ('I will atone with my blood — the love which I placed in you') — ponderous, gory, heavy words, with the fugitive, watery words (*'J'ai froid — ta chevelure'*) of *Pelléas et Mélisande*.

I began to wonder if that (*Pelléas et Mélisande*) were not the beginning of our silence.

Because silence must be numbered among the strangest and gravest vices of our time. Those of us who have tried to write novels in our time know the discomfort and unhappiness that appears as soon as we reach the point when we have to make our characters talk to one another. For page after page our characters exchange comments that are insignificant but pregnant with a desolate unhappiness: 'Are you cold?' 'No, I'm not cold.' 'Would you like some tea?' 'No thanks.' 'Are you tired?' 'I don't know. Yes, perhaps I'm a bit tired.' This is how our characters talk. They talk like this to kill time. They talk like this because they don't know how to talk any more. Little by little the most important matters, the most terrible confessions, come out: 'You killed him?' 'Yes, I killed him.' The meagre barren words of our time are painfully wrung from silence and appear like the signals of castaways, beacons lit on the most distant hills, weak, desperate summonses that are swallowed up in space.

And so when we want to make our characters talk, we measure the profound silence that has, little by little, built up within us. We began to be silent as children, at table, in front of our parents who still spoke to us using the old, heavy, gory words. We remained silent. We remained silent as a protest and as a mark of contempt. We remained silent so that our parents would realize that their ponderous words were no longer any use to us. We had others that we kept in reserve. We would use these new words of ours later, with people who would understand them. Our silence was our wealth. Now we are ashamed of it and desperate and we know all the misery it brings. We shall never be free of it again. Those ponderous words that served our parents are a currency that has been withdrawn and which no one accepts. And we realize that the new words have no value, that we can buy nothing with them. They are no use for establishing relationships, they are watery, cold, sterile. They are no use for writing books, for linking us with someone we love, for saving a friend.

It is well known that a feeling of guilt is one of the vices of our time; a great deal is talked and written about it. We all suffer from it. We feel ourselves to be involved with something that gets filthier with every day that passes. And there is also the feeling of panic; we all suffer from that too. The feeling of panic comes from the feeling of guilt. And a man who is panic-stricken and guilty stays silent.

Everyone looks in his own way for something that will cure the silence, the feeling of guilt, the feeling of panic. Some people travel. In their anxiety to see new countries and new people there is the hope that they will leave behind their own obscure ghosts; there is the secret hope that somewhere on the earth they will find the one person who could talk to them. Some people get drunk in order to forget their own obscure ghosts, and to talk. And then there are all the things people do *so that they do not have to talk*: some people spend their evenings stretched out in the cinema with a woman beside them to whom, in this way, they don't have to talk; some people learn how to play bridge; some people make love, which can also be done without talking.. Usually they say they are doing these things *to kill time*; in fact they do them to kill the silence.

There are two kinds of silence; silence with oneself and silence with others. Both kinds make us suffer equally. The silence with ourselves is dominated by a violent dislike for our own existence, by a contempt for our own soul which seems so vile that it is not worth speaking to. Clearly we have to break this silence with ourselves if we wish to try and break the silence with others. Clearly we have no right to hate ourselves, no right to say nothing about our thoughts to our own souls.

The commonest way of freeing oneself from silence is to be psychoanalysed. To talk endlessly about oneself to a person who listens, who is paid to listen: to uncover the roots of our own silence: yes, this can give some momentary relief. But the silence is profound and universal. We rediscover it as soon as we have left the room in which that person, paid to listen, listened to us. We immediately sink into it again. And then this hour's relief seems superficial and banal to us. Silence is worldwide: someone who cures it in one of us for one hour does nothing towards solving the common problem.

When we go to be psychoanalysed we are told that we must stop hating ourselves so violently. But in order to free us from this hatred, to free us from this guilt, this feeling of panic, this silence, we are told that we must live according to nature, that we must indulge our instincts, that we must follow our own desires: that we must make a free choice of our lives. But to make a free choice of your life is not to live according to nature; it is to live unnaturally, because man is not always given a free choice: he does not choose the hour of his birth, or his face, or his parents, or his childhood; he does not normally choose the hour of his death. A man has no choice but to accept his face as he has no choice but to accept his destiny: and the only choice he is permitted is the choice between good and evil, between justice and injustice, between truth and lies. The things they tell those of us who go to be psychoanalysed are of no use to us because they do not take our moral responsibility — which is the only choice permitted us in life — into account; those of us who have been psychoanalysed know only too well how rarefied, unnatural and finally unbreathable is that atmosphere of ephemeral freedom in which we live just as we wish.

Usually this vice of silence that poisons our epoch is summed up by a cliché, 'We have lost the art of conversation'. This is the frivolous, commonplace expression of a real and tragic truth. When we say 'the art of conversation' we are not saying anything that helps us to live; what we lack is the opportunity of free, normal relationships between men, and we miss it to such an extent that some of us are driven to suicide by our awareness of this absence. Every day silence harvests its victims. Silence is a mortal illness.

Today, as never before, the fates of men are so intimately linked to one another that a disaster for one is a disaster for everybody. It is strange but true that men find themselves intimately linked to one another's destinies to such an extent that the fall of one sweeps away thousands of others, and at the same time they are all smothered by silence, incapable of exchanging a single unconstrained word. For this reason — because one person's disaster is everyone's disaster — the ways of curing this silence that have been suggested to us are clearly unreal. We have been advised to defend ourselves from despair with egotism. But egotism has never solved despair. And we are too used to calling our soul's vices *illnesses*, to putting up with them and to letting them rule our lives, or to soothing them with sweet syrups in order to cure them as if they were illnesses. Silence must be faced and judged from a moral standpoint. It is not given to us to choose whether we are happy or unhappy. But we *must* choose not to be *demonically* unhappy. Silence can become a closed, monstrous, *demonic* unhappiness: it withers the days of our youth and makes our bread bitter. It can lead, as I have said, to death.

Silence must be faced and judged from a moral standpoint. Because silence, like acedia and like luxury, is a sin. The fact that in our time it is a sin common to all our fellow men, that it is the bitter fruit of our sick times, does not excuse us from recognizing it for what it is and from calling it by its true name.

# Human Relationships

The problem of our relationships with other human beings lies at the centre of our life: as soon as we become aware of this — that is, as soon as we clearly see it as a problem and no longer as the muddle of unhappiness, we start to look for its origins, and to reconstruct its course throughout our whole life.

When we are little children we have our eyes fixed above all on the world of adults, which is dark and mysterious to us. It seems absurd to us because we don't understand any of the words which adults say to one another, or the sense of their decisions and actions, or the reasons for their changes of mood and sudden outbursts of anger. We don't understand the words which adults say to each other and we are not interested in them; on the contrary they are infinitely boring to us. What interests us are the decisions of theirs that can alter our daily routine, the black moods that spoil lunches and suppers, the sudden slamming of doors, and voices raised in the night. We realize that at any moment an unexpected storm — complete with the sound of doors being slammed and objects being hurled about — can irrupt from a few quiet words. We nervously listen for the slightest indication of violence in the voices that are talking. We can be alone and absorbed in play when, suddenly, angry voices are raised in the house: we go on playing mechanically, pushing pebbles and grass into a little heap of earth to make a hill: but we are no longer interested in the little hill because we know that we cannot be happy until the house is at peace again; doors slam and we jump; angry words fly from one room to another — words that are incomprehensible to us and we do not try to understand them or discover the murky reasons for their existence, we vaguely think that whatever reasons there may be must be horrible; we are so weighed down by all the absurd mystery of adult life. And sometimes this complicates our relationships with other children, with the world of our equals: sometimes we have a friend with us who has come to play; we are making a little hill with him when a slammed door tells us that peace is at an end; burning with shame we pretend to be extremely interested in the little hill, we do our utmost to distract our friend's attention from the brutal voices that are re-echoing through the house; with hands that are suddenly sweaty and tired we precisely push our little bits of wood into the heap of earth. We are absolutely certain that no one ever argues or screams brutal words at one another in our friend's house; in our friend's house everyone is calm and cultured, and arguing is a shame peculiar to our house; then one day we discover with immense relief that they argue in our friend's house just as they do in our house, as they do perhaps in every house on earth.

We become adolescents when the words that adults exchange with one another become intelligible to us; intelligible, but of no interest because we no longer care whether peace reigns in the house or not. Now we are able to follow the ins and outs of family rows and to foresee their course and how long they will last; and we are not afraid of them anymore, doors slam and we do not jump. The house is no longer what it was for us before, it is no longer the point from which we look out on the rest of the universe, it is a place where — by chance — we eat and live: we eat quickly, lending one inattentive ear to the adults' conversation — a conversation which is intelligible to us but which strikes us as useless; we eat and quickly escape to our rooms so that we don't have to listen to their useless conversation; and we are able to be perfectly happy even if the adults around us are arguing and sulking day in day out. The things that matter to us no longer happen within the walls of our house but outside, in the street and at school; we feel that we cannot be happy if the other children at school look down on us in any way. We would do anything to escape their contempt; and we do anything. We write comic verses to amuse our friends, which we recite to them with ridiculous grimaces that we are ashamed of afterwards; we collect obscene words so that they will think well of us, we go looking all day long for obscene words in the books and dictionaries that we have in the house; and because it seems to us that a showy, gaudy way of dressing is popular with our friends we (against our mother's wishes) try to add something that is a bit showy and vulgar to our quiet clothes. We vaguely feel that if we are looked down on it is above all because we are shy: who knows, perhaps that moment long ago when we were making a little heap of earth with our friend and the doors slammed and brutal voices re-echoed and shame burnt our cheeks, perhaps it was that moment which planted the roots of shyness in us: and we think that our whole life will have to be spent in freeing ourselves from this shyness, in learning to move under the gaze of others with the same self-confidence and carelessness as when we are alone. We think of our shyness as the most important obstacle to winning sympathy and universal approbation: and we are hungry and thirsty for this approbation: in our lonely daydreams we see ourselves riding trimphantly on horseback through a city, in the midst of an applauding, adoring crowd.

At home we punish the adults — whose absurdly mysterious ways weighed us down for so many years — with our profound contempt, with our taciturn, impenetrable faces; their mystery has obsessed us for so many years, and now we take our revenge by confronting them with our mystery, a silent impenetrable face and eyes of stone. And we also take revenge on the adults at home for the contempt shown us by other school-children. It seems to us that this contempt includes not only us but our whole family, our social position, the furnishings in our home, our parents' habits and behaviour. Every now and then anger erupts in the house as of old, but now it is directed at us, at our stony faces: a whirlwind of violent language breaks over us; doors slam but we do not jump; now the doors slam because of us as we sit unmoving at the table, with a disdainful smile: later on, alone in our room, our disdainful smile suddenly melts away and we burst into tears and daydream about our loneliness and how the others do not understand us; and we feel strangely happy to be pouring out these scalding tears and stifling our sobs in a cushion. Then mother arrives and is touched at the sight of our tears and offers to take us out for an ice-cream or to the cinema; with our red, swollen eyes, but stony-faced and impenetrable again, we sit next to mother at a little table in a café, eating ice-cream with a tiny spoon; all around us moves a crowd of people who are apparently calm and light-hearted while we, oh we are the gloomiest, most gauche and detestable thing on earth.

'Who are the others and who are we?' we wonder. Sometimes we stay alone in our room for a whole afternoon, thinking; with a vague feeling of dizziness we wonder whether the others really exist at all, or if it is we who have invented them. We say that perhaps when we are not there all the others cease to exist and disappear in an instant; and miraculously reassemble, suddenly appearing from the earth, as soon as we look at them. Isn't it possible that one day when we turn round unexpectedly we shall find nothing, no one, and be left staring into emptiness? And so there's no reason, we say, to get so upset about the others' contempt, because perhaps the others don't exist and therefore think neither about us nor about themselves. While we are absorbed in these dizzying thoughts mother comes and suggests we go out for an ice-cream; and we feel inexplicably happy, excessively happy, thinking about the ice-cream that we are going to eat in a little while; and however has the prospect of an ice-cream made us so happy we wonder, we who are so adult, with our dizzying thoughts, who are so strangely lost in a world of shadows? We agree to mother's suggestion, but we are careful not to show her how happy we are about it; our lips are sealed as we walk to the café with her.

Though we constantly tell ourselves that perhaps the others do not exist, that it is we who have invented them, we inexplicably continue to suffer from the contempt shown to us by our schoolfellows, and from our heaviness and clumsiness which we ourselves find shamefully contemptible; when others talk to us our face feels so ugly and shapeless that we want to cover it with our hands; and yet we are always daydreaming that someone will fall in love with us, that he sees us in the café while we are having an ice-cream with mother, that he secretly follows us home and writes us a love-letter; we wait for this letter and every day we are extremely surprised that we haven't received it yet; we have murmured its phrases so often that we know them by heart, and when this letter does arrive we really shall have a marvellous mystery that is nothing to do with home, a secret intrigue whose ramifications are entirely outside the house; because we have to confess that at the moment our mystery is a poor thing and that behind the stony mask which we offer to our parents for their goodnight kiss we are hiding very little; after that kiss we hurry to our room while our parents whisper suspicious questions about us.

In the morning we go to school after having stared concentratedly at our face in the mirror: our face has lost the soft delicacy of childhood; now we think regretfully about childhood and when we made little heaps of earth and our only unhappiness was when there was quarrelling in the house: now they do not quarrel so often in the house — our elder brothers have gone off to live their own lives, our parents have become older and quieter; but now we don't care about the house; we walk to school alone in the mist; when we were little mother came to school with us and came to collect us; now we are alone in the mist and terribly responsible for everything we do.

God has said 'Love thy neighbour as thyself'. This seems absurd to us; God has said something absurd, he has imposed on man something that is impossible to carry out. How can we love our neighbour when he despises us and won't let us love him? And how can we love ourselves — disgusting and heavy and gloomy as we are? How can we love our neighbour who perhaps doesn't exist and is only a crowd of shadows while God has created us, only us, and placed us on an earth that is a shadow where we live on our dizzying thoughts? We have believed in God since we were little, but now we think that perhaps he doesn't exist, or he exists and doesn't care about us because he has placed us in such cruel circumstances, and so for us it is as if he didn't exist. Then at table we refuse some dish we particularly like and we pass the night stretched out on the rug in our room in order to mortify ourselves and punish ourselves for our hateful thoughts, and be loved by God.

'But God does not exist' we think, after an entire night shivering on the floor with our limbs numbed by cold and sleep. God does not exist because he could not have invented this absurd, monstrous world, this complicated contrivance in which a human being walks alone in the fog each morning, between high houses inhabited by his neighbour who does not love him and who is impossible to love. And that monstrous inexplicable race who are of a different sex from us and who possess a terrible ability to do everything good and everything evil to us, who have a terrible secret power over us, they are also our neighbour. Could we ever be attractive to that other race, we who are so despised by our companions of our own sex, who are considered to be so boring and empty, so useless and clumsy at everything?

Then one day it happens that the most admired, the most sought after of all our school-fellows, the top of the class, suddenly becomes friends with us. How this has come about we do not know. She suddenly fixed her blue eyes on us, walked home with us and began to think well of us. In the afternoon she comes to our house to do her homework; in our hands we hold the precious exercise book belonging to the top of the class, with her beautiful angular handwriting in blue ink: we can copy her homework which has no mistakes in it. How has such happiness come to us? How have we acquired this friend, who is so proud with everyone and so unapproachable? Now she wanders within the walls of our room, shaking her mane of red hair beside us, leaning her sharp profile — which is covered in pinkish freckles — over the familiar objects in our room: it seems to us that some rare tropical animal has miraculously been domesticated and appeared within the walls of our house. She wanders around our room, asks where things come from, asks if she can borrow some book or other; she has tea with us, and she spits plum stones off the terrace with us. We who were despised by everyone have been chosen by the most unapproachable, the most unexpected companion. We talk to her convulsively so that she will not be bored by our company, so that she will not leave us forever: in a rush we tell her all our obscene words and everything we know about films and sport. When we are alone we say the syllables of her beautiful sonorous name over and over again, and we prepare a thousand things to say to her the next day; we are wild with happiness and begin to imagine that she is like us in every way; the next day we try the speeches we have prepared on her, we tell her everything about our life, even our dizzying suspicion that neither people nor things exist: she looks at us uneasily, giggles, and makes fun of us a little. Then we realize that we have made a mistake and that it is not possible to talk to her about this subject; we fall back on obscene words and sport.

Meanwhile, our situation at school has changed overnight: everyone begins to respect us when they see that we are respected by the most respected person in the group; the comic verses we have written 'and which we now recite are received with shrieks of shrill applause: before, we could not make our voice heard above the general hubbub of voices, now everyone listens in silence when we speak; now they ask us questions and walk arm in arm with us, they help us with the things we are less good at, like sports or homework we don't know how to do. The world no longer appears to us as a monstrous contrivance but like a simple, smiling little island populated with friends: we do not thank God for such a lucky change in our fortunes because we no longer think about God; it seems impossible to us to think about anything except the cheerful faces of our friends gathered around us, the way the mornings flow happily and easily past, the crazy things we have said that made everyone laugh; and our face in the mirror is no longer something gloomy and shapeless but the face which our friends greet happily every morning. Sustained in this way by the friendship of companions of our own sex, we look with less horror at that other race, the people of a different sex from ours; it almost seems to us that we could easily do without this different race, that we could be happy without their approbation; we almost wish we could spend our whole life surrounded by school friends, saying crazy things and making them laugh.

Then little by little we discover one friend, in the midst of the crowd of friends, who is particularly happy to be with us and to whom, we realize, we have an infinite number of things to say. She is not the top of the class, she is not particularly well thought of by the others, she does not wear showy clothes: in fact her clothes are made of fine, warm cloth very like that which our mother chooses for us; and when we are walking home with her we realize that her shoes are identical to ours — strong and simple, not showy and flimsy like those of our other friends; we laughingly point this out to her. Little by little we find out that the same habits prevail in her house as in ours: and that she bathes often, and that her mother does not let her go to see romantic films just as our mother doesn't allow us to. She is a person like us; she is from the same social background. By this time we are very fed up with the company of the top of the class who still comes to see us every afternoon; by this time we are fed up with repeating the same old obscene words and now we proudly confront the top of the class with remarks about the subject that interests us, our doubts about existence; we do this so disdainfully and carelessly, and with such pride, that the top of the class doesn't really understand us, but smiles shyly; we see that shy, cowardly smile on her lips; she is afraid of losing us. We are no longer bewitched by her blue eyes, and when we are with her we long for the round, hazel eyes of our other friend; and the top of the class realizes this and is upset by it, and we are proud of making her upset; and so we too are capable of making someone suffer.

With our new friend who has round eyes, we despise the top of the class and our other friends who are so noisy and vulgar, with all their obscene words that they are always repeating: now we wish to be very refined, with our new friend we judge people and things according to criteria of refinement or vulgarity. We discover that it is refined to stay children as long as possible; to the great relief of our mothers we give up all the vulgar showy things we had added to our clothes; in our clothes as in our demeanour and habits we look for a childlike simplicity. We spend extraordinary afternoons with our new friend; we are never weary of talking and listening. We are astonished when we think of our friendship with the top of the class whom we have now stopped seeing; being with the top of the class became so tiring that in the end we felt our eyelids smarting, our skin itching and the muscles of our face aching with the effort of keeping up our false smile; it was tiring to hide our dislike, to suppress confidences, to constantly choose those few words that could be said to the top of the class; being with our new friend is so pleasant, we have nothing to hide or suppress and we can let our words flow freely. We even confide our dizzying suspicions about existence to her: and then she tells us with astonishment that she has had the same suspicions: 'but do you exist?' we ask her, and she swears that she exists, and we are infinitely happy.

We and our new friend are sorry that we are of the same sex, because if we were of different sexes we could get married so that we would be together for ever and ever. We have no fear of each other, or shame, or horror: and so a shadow hangs over our life which could now have been so happy — the uncertainty as to whether one day someone of the opposite sex will be able to love us. People of the opposite sex walk next to us, brush against us in the street, perhaps think about us or have designs on us which we can never know; they have our fate — our happiness — in their hands. Perhaps the person who is suitable for us, who could love us and whom we could love, is among them: the person who is right for us; but where? How can we recognize this person, how can we make him recognize us, in the crowded city? In which house in the city, at which point on the earth, does this person live who is right for us, who is like us in every way, who is ready to answer all our questions, ready to listen to us for ever without getting bored, to smile at our faults, to live with our face all his life? What words ought we to say so that he will recognize us among thousands? How should we dress, what places should we go in order to meet him?

We are tormented by these thoughts and when we are with people of the opposite sex we feel extremely shy because we are afraid that one of them could be the right person for us and we could lose him with a word. We think carefully about all our words before uttering them and then we say them hurriedly, in a strangled voice; because of our fear we glance about gloomily and have tiny, abrupt gestures; we are aware of all this but we tell ourselves that the person who has been made for us must recognize us even though we have these abrupt gestures and this strangled voice: if he doesn't give any sign of having noticed us it is because he is not the right person; the right person will recognize us and pick us out among thousands. We wait for the right person; every morning when we get up we think that this could be the day when we meet him; we dress and comb our hair with infinite care, and overcome the desire to go out in an old raincoat and shapeless shoes; the right person might just happen to be on the corner of the street. Thousands and thousands of times we think that we are in the presence of the person made for us: our hearts beats tumultuously at the sound of a particular name, at the curve of a nose or a smile, and only because we have suddenly decided that this is the nose and the name and the smile of the person made for us: a car with yellow wheels and an old lady make us blush uncontrollably because we think them the car and the mother of the right person for us — the car in which we will set off on our honeymoon, the mother who will have to place her hand on us in benediction. All at once we realize we have made a mistake — that wasn't the right person, he is of no interest to us whatsoever,

and we don't suffer because we have no time to suffer;
suddenly the car with yellow wheels, the name and the
smile fade away and are absorbed into the thousand
useless things that surround our life. But we don't have
time to suffer; we are leaving for a holiday in the country
and we are absolutely certain that during these holidays
we shall meet the right person; because we are convinced
that the train will take us to the right person we are more
or less unmoved by parting from our friend with the
round eyes; and she for her part is convinced of the same
thing: goodness knows why we are suddenly convinced
that the right person will be met on a summer holiday in
the country. The long, lonely, boring months pass by:
we write interminable letters to our friend and to console
ourselves for the meeting that never happens we carefully
collect together all the favourable judgements passed on
us by old acquaintances of the family or by aged relatives
and write them out for our friend; she writes to us similar
letters containing the favourable judgements on her
intelligence and beauty passed by her aged relatives.
When autumn comes we have to admit inwardly that
nothing extraordinary has happened; but we are not
disappointed, we eagerly rejoin our friend and our other
companions and contentedly settle down to the autumn;
the right person is waiting for us, perhaps, at the corner
of the avenue.

Then little by little we withdraw from our friend. We
find her a bit boring, 'bourgeois'; she is always obsessed
with elegance and refinement. Now we want to be poor:
we become involved with a group of poor friends and
every day we proudly go to their unheated house. We
wear our old raincoat now, and with pride: we still count
on meeting the right person, but he must love our old
raincoat, he must love our shapeless shoes, our cheap
cigarettes and our bare, red hands. Dressed in our old
raincoat we walk alone at dusk past the houses on the
edge of the city; we have discovered the edge of the city,

the signboards of the little cafés beside the river, and we linger lost in thought in front of little shops where long pink bodices are hung up, and workmen's overalls, and coffee-coloured underpants; we stand gaping in front of a shop window of old postcards and old hairpins: we like everything that is old, dusty and poor: we go searching through the city for poor, dusty things. Meanwhile it pours with rain onto our old raincoat, which lets water through, and on to our uncovered head; we don't have an umbrella — we would rather commit suicide than go out with an umbrella; we don't have an umbrella or a hat or gloves or the tram fare: all we have is a dirty handkerchief in our pocket, and some crushed cigarettes and kitchen matches.

Suddenly it occurs to us that the poor are our neighbour, the poor are the neighbour whom we have to love; we watch the poor as they pass by us; we look out for a chance to take a blind beggar across the road, to offer our arm to some old lady who has slipped in a puddle; we shyly caress — with the tips of our fingers — the filthy hair of children playing in the alleyways; we return home soaked to the skin, chilled to the marrow, and triumphant. We are not poor, we do not spend the night on a bench in a public park, we do not drink cloudy soup from a tin saucepan; we are not poor, but only by chance: we shall be extremely poor tomorrow.

Meanwhile the friend whom we have stopped seeing suffers on our account, just as the top of the class suffered when we stopped seeing her. We know this, but we don't feel sorry about it; it even gives us a kind of underhand pleasure, because if someone suffers on our account it means that we — who for so long thought of ourselves as weak and insignificant — have in our hands the power to make someone suffer. We don't suspect that we are perhaps cynical and wicked because we don't suspect that our friend is also our neighbour: neither do we think that our parents are our neighbour: our neighbour is the poor.

We give our parents severe looks as they eat their good food at their well-lit table; we also eat this good food, but we think that this is by chance, and it will only be like this for a very short time: in a little while we will have nothing more than a bit of black bread and a tin saucepan.

One day we meet the right person. We are unmoved, because we haven't recognized him; we walk with the right person along the streets at the edge of the city, and little by little we fall into the habit of walking together every day. From time to time we wonder absent-mindedly whether we are not perhaps walking with the right person, but we think that probably we are not. We are too calm; the earth and the sky are unchanged, the minutes and hours flow quietly on without awakening any deep echo in our heart. We have been mistaken so often; we believed we were in the presence of the right person and we weren't. And in the presence of each wrong right person we were impetuously swept away in such a tumult of emotion that we scarcely had strength left to think; we found ourselves living at the centre of a landscape on fire; trees, houses and objects burst into flames around us. And then all at once the fire had died down and there was nothing left but a few warm embers: there are so many burnt out landscapes behind us that we cannot even count them. Now nothing around us is on fire. For weeks and months we spend our days with the right person without realizing; only sometimes, the thought of the curve of his lips, of certain of his gestures and the intonation of his voice, produces a slight tremor in our heart: but we don't think anything of such a slight, muffled tremor. The strange thing is that when we are with this person we always feel so well and at peace, able to breathe deeply, and our forehead which has been so wrinkled and grim for so long is suddenly smooth again; and we never tire of talking and listening. We realize that we have never had a relationship like this with any other human being; in time all human beings had seemed so inoffensive, so simple and small to us: but when we walk beside this person with his pace that is different from ours, and his severe profile, he has an infinite capacity to do to us everything that is good and everything that is evil. And yet we feel infinitely calm.

And we leave home and go to live with this person for ever; not because we are sure that he is the right person: in fact we are not entirely sure, and we always suspect that the right person for us is hiding away goodness knows where in the city. But we don't want to know where he is hiding; we feel that we have by now very little to say to him, because we say everything to this person — who is not perhaps the right person — with whom we now live; and we want to receive the good and the evil of our lives from this person and with him. Every now and then violent differences between us and this person erupt into the open; and yet they are unable to destroy the infinite peace we have within us. After many years, only after many years, after a thick web of habits, memories and violent differences has been woven between us, we at last realize that he is, in truth, the right person for us, that we could not have put up with anyone else, that it is only from him that we can ask everything that the heart needs.

Now, in the new house where we have come to live, and that is ours, we don't want to be poor, in fact we are a little afraid of poverty: we feel a strange affection for the objects around us, for a table or for a rug — we, who were always spilling ink on our parents' rugs; this new affection of ours for a rug bothers us a little, we are a bit ashamed of it; sometimes we still go for walks at the edge of the city, but when we come home we carefully clean our muddy shoes on the doormat; and we feel a new kind of peace when we sit at home, under the lamp, with the shutters closed against the dark city. We no longer want friends very much, because we tell the person who lives with us all our thoughts, while we are eating soup at our well-lit table; it doesn't seem worth the effort to tell other people anything.

Our children are born, and the fear of poverty grows in us; indeed an endless number of fears — of every danger or kind of suffering that could attack our children's mortal flesh and blood — grows in us. In the past we never thought of our own flesh and blood, our own body, as being frail and mortal: we were ready to hurl ourselves into the most unexpected adventures, we were always about to set off for the most distant places to live among lepers and cannibals; every possibility of wars and epidemics and cosmic catastrophes left us quite unmoved. We did not know that there could be such fear, such frailty, in our body: we never suspected that we could feel so bound to life by a chain of fear, of such heart-rending tenderness. How strong and free our past was, when we walked alone at will through the city! We felt such pity for the families we saw; the fathers and mothers with their prams out for a careful little Sunday stroll along the avenues seemed to us to be something so tedious and sad. Now we are one of those families, we go carefully along the avenues pushing our pram and we are not sad, in fact we could be said to be happy, though it is a happiness that is difficult to recognize in the midst of our panic that we could from one moment to the next lose it for ever: the baby in the pram we are pushing is so small, so weak, the love which binds us to him is so painful, so frightening! We are afraid of a breath of wind, of a cloud in the sky; isn't it going to rain? We — who have been soaked and bareheaded with our feet in the puddles so often! Now we have an umbrella. And we would like to have an umbrella stand in the house, in the hall; the strangest desires come to us, desires we would never have dreamed we could have when we walked through the city alone and free; we would like an umbrella-stand and a coat-rack, towels, a camping oven, a refrigerator. We don't go to the edge of the city anymore; we go through the avenues, between villas and gardens; we are careful that our children have no contact with people who are particularly dirty or poor because we are afraid of lice and diseases; we flee from beggars.

We love our children in such a painful, frightening way that it seems to us we have never had any other neighbour, that we never could have any other. We are still not very used to our children's presence on the earth; we are still bemused and bewildered by their sudden appearance in life. We no longer have friends; or rather if our child is ill we think with loathing of those few friends we do have — it almost seems to us to be their fault because whilst we are in their company we are distracted from this unique heart-rending tenderness: we no longer have a vocation: we had a vocation, a profession that was dear to us, and now as soon as we give it half our attention we feel guilty and rush back to this unique, heart-rending tenderness; a sunny day, a green landscape, signify for us only that our baby can get brown in the sun or play on the grass; we have lost every ability to think of ourselves or enjoy ourselves. We gaze at everything in a worried, suspicious way, we look to see that there are no rusty nails or cockroaches or other dangers for our baby. We want to live in clean, fresh countries, with clean animals and kindly people; the brutal universe that used to fascinate us does not fascinate us any more.

And how stupid we have become, we occasionally and regretfully think, as we look at our baby's head which is so familiar, familiar to us in a way that nothing else in the world has ever been, as we watch him while he is sitting making a little hill of earth with his pudgy fingers. How stupid, and small, and sluggish our thoughts have become, so small that they could be packed into a nut-shell, and yet at the same time so tiring and suffocating! Where has the brutal universe that fascinated us gone, and where have the strength and vitality and freedom of our youth gone, and our eager discovery of things day by day, our resolute glorious gaze, our triumphant past? Where is our neighbour now? Where is God now? We only remember to talk to God when our baby is ill: then we tell him to make all our teeth and hair drop out but to make our baby better. As soon as the baby is better we forget about God; we still have our teeth and hair and we resume our petty, tiring, sluggish thoughts again — rusty nails, cockroaches, fresh pastures, gruel. We have become superstitious too and are always warding off bad luck — we are sitting working, writing away, when suddenly we get up and put the light on and off three times in order to ward off bad luck because out of the blue we felt that only this would save us from a catastrophe. We refuse to suffer; we hear suffering approach us and we hide behind the armchair, behind the curtains, so that it won't find us.

But then suffering comes to us. We have expected it, but we don't recognize it at first: we don't call it by its real name at first. Stunned and incredulous, trusting that everything can be put right, we descend the steps of our house and close its door for ever; we walk through interminable dusty streets. They follow us and we hide; we hide in convents and in woods, in barns and in alleyways, in the holds of ships and in cellars. We learn to ask for help from the first passer-by; we don't know if he is a friend or an enemy, if he will want to help us or betray us; but we have no choice, and for a moment we trust our life to him. We also learn to give help to the first passer-by. And we always keep alive our faith that in a while, in a few hours or a few days, we shall go back to our house with its rugs and lamps; we shall be comforted and consoled; our children will sit down to play with clean aprons on and red slippers. We sleep with our children in stations, on the steps of churches, in the doss-houses of the poor; we are poor, we think, but without any pride; little by little every trace of our childish pride disappears. We are really hungry and really cold. We no longer feel fear; fear has penetrated into us, it is one with our exhaustion; it is the arid, uncaring gaze with which we stare at things.

But at intervals, from the depths of our exhaustion, the awareness of things rises up in us again, and it is so sharp that it moves us to tears; perhaps we are looking at the earth for the last time. We have never before felt with such force the love that binds us to the dust in the street, to the high calls of the birds, to the laboured rhythm of our breathing: but we sense that we are stronger than that laboured rhythm, it seems so muffled within us, so distant, as if it were no longer ours. We have never loved our children so much, their weight in our arms, the touch of their hair on our cheeks; and yet we do not even feel fear for our children: we say to God that he will protect them if he wishes. We tell him to do as he wishes.

And now we are really adult we think one morning, as we look in the mirror at our lined, furrowed face; we look at it without pride, without any curiosity; with a little compassion. Once again we have a mirror within four walls: who knows, perhaps in a little while we shall also have a rug again, a lamp perhaps. But we have lost those who are dearest to us, and so what can rugs and red slippers mean to us? We learn to conceal and look after the objects that belonged to the dead; to go alone to the places where we went with them; to ask questions and hear the silence around us. We no longer fear death; every hour, every minute, we look at death and remember its great silence on the face that was dearest to us.

And now we are really adult we think, and we are astonished that this is what being an adult is — not in truth everything we believed as a child, not in truth self-confidence, not in truth the calm ownership of every-thing on earth. We are adult because we have behind us the silent presence of the dead, whom we ask to judge our current actions and from whom we ask forgiveness for past offences: we should like to uproot from our past so many cruel words, so many cruel acts that we committed when, though we feared death, we did not know — we had not yet understood — how irreperable, how irremediable, death is: we are adult because of the silent answers, because of all the silent forgiveness of the dead which we carry within us. We are adult because of that brief moment when one day it fell to our lot to live when we had looked at the things of the world as if for the last time, when we had renounced our possession of them and returned them to the will of God: and suddenly the things of the world appeared to us in their just place beneath the sky, and the human beings too, and we who looked at them from the just place that is given to us: human beings, objects and memories — everything appeared to us in its just place beneath the sky. In that brief moment we found a point of equilibrium for our wavering life: and it seemed to us that we could always rediscover that secret moment and find there the words for our vocation, the words for our neighbour; that we could look at our neighbour with a gaze that would always be just and free, not the timid or contemptuous gaze of someone who whenever he is with his neighbour always asks himself if he is his master or his servant. All our life we have only known how to be masters and servants: but in that secret moment of ours, in our moment of perfect equilibrium, we have realized that there is no real authority or servitude on the earth. And so it is that now as we turn to that secret moment we look at others to see whether they have lived through an identical moment, or whether they are still far away from it; it is this that we have to know. It is the highest moment in the life of a human being, and it is necessary that we stand with others whose eyes are fixed on the highest moment of their destiny.

We realize with astonishment that now we are adult we have not lost our old shyness when we are with our neighbour: life has not helped us to free ourselves from this shyness at all. We are still shy. Only, it doesn't matter; it seems that our claim to be shy has been conquered for us; we are shy without shyness, boldly shy. We shyly search within us for the right words. We are very pleased to find them, shyly but as it were without any trouble; we are pleased that we have so many words within us, so many words for our neighbour that we seem intoxicated with our own ease and naturalness. And the story of human relationships never ceases for us; because little by little they become all too easy for us, all too natural and spontaneous — so spontaneous and so undemanding that there is no richness, discovery or choice about them; they are just habit and complacency, a kind of intoxicated naturalness. We believe that we can always return to that secret moment of ours, that we can draw on the right words; but it isn't true that we can always go back there, often our return there is false; we make our eyes glow with a false light, we pretend to be caring and warm towards our neighbour and we are in fact once more shrunken and hunched up in the icy darkness of our heart. Human relationships have to be rediscovered and reinvented every day. We have to remember constantly that every kind of meeting with our neighbour is a human action and so it is always evil or good, true or deceitful, a kindness or a sin.

Now we are so adult that our adolescent children have already started to look at us with eyes of stone; we are upset by it, even though we know only too well what that stare means; even though we remember only too well having stared in the same way. We are upset by it and we complain about it and whisper our suspicious questions, even though by now we know how the long chain of human relationships unwinds its long necessary parabola, and though we know all the long road we have to travel down in order to arrive at the point where we have a little compassion.

# The Little Virtues

As far as the education of children is concerned I think they should be taught not the little virtues but the great ones. Not thrift but generosity and an indifference to money; not caution but courage and a contempt for danger; nor shrewdness but frankness and a love of truth; not tact but love for one's neighbour and self-denial; not a desire for success but a desire to be and to know.

Usually we do just the opposite; we rush to teach them a respect for the little virtues, on which we build our whole system of education. In doing this we are choosing the easiest way, because the little virtues do not involve any actual dangers, indeed they provide shelter from Fortune's blows. We do not bother to teach the great virtues, though we love them and want our children to have them; but we nourish the hope that they will spontaneously appear in their consciousness some day in the future, we think of them as being part of our instinctive nature, while the others, the little virtues, seem to be the result of reflection and calculation and so we think that they absolutely must be taught.

In reality the difference is only an apparent one. The little virtues also arise from our deepest instincts, from a defensive instinct; but in them reason speaks, holds forth, displays its arguments as the brilliant advocate of self-preservation. The great virtues well up from an instinct in which reason does not speak, an instinct that seems to be difficult to name. And the best of us is in that silent instinct, and not in our defensive instinct which harangues, holds forth and displays its arguments with reason's voice.

Education is only a certain relationship which we establish between ourselves and our children, a certain climate in which feelings, instincts and thoughts can flourish. Now I believe that a climate which is completely pervaded by a respect for the little virtues will, insensibly, lead to cynicism or to a fear of life. In themselves the little virtues have nothing to do with cynicism or a fear of life, but taken together, and without the great virtues, they produce an atmosphere that leads to these consequences. Not that the little virtues are in themselves contemptible; but their value is of a complementary and not of a substantial kind; they cannot stand by themselves without the others, and by themselves and without the others they provide but meagre fare for human nature. By looking around himself a man can find out how to use the little virtues — moderately and when they are necessary — he can drink them in from the air, because the little virtues are of a kind that is common among men. But one cannot breathe in the great virtues from the surrounding air, and they should be the basis of our relationship with our children, the first foundation of their education. Besides, the great can also contain the little, but by the laws of nature there is no way that the little can contain the great.

In our relationships with our children it is no use our trying to remember and imitate the way our parents acted with us. The time of our youth and childhood was not one of little virtues; it was a time of strong and sonorous words that little by little lost all their substance. The present is a time of cold, submissive words beneath which a desire for reassertion is perhaps coming to the surface. But it is a timid desire that is afraid of ridicule. And so we hide behind caution and shrewdness. Our parents knew neither caution nor shrewdness and they didn't know the fear of ridicule either: they were illogical and incoherent but they never realized this; they constantly contradicted themselves but they never allowed anyone to contradict them. They were authoritarian towards us in a way that we are quite incapable of being. Strong in their principles, which they believed to be indestructible, they reigned over us with absolute power. They deafened us with their thunderous words: a dialogue was impossible because as soon as they suspected that they were wrong they ordered us to be quiet: they beat their fists on the table and made the room shake. We remember that gesture but we cannot copy it. We can fly into a rage and howl like wolves, but deep in our wolf's howl there lies a hysterical sob, the hoarse bleating of a lamb.

And so we have no authority; we have no weapons. Authority in us would be a hypocrisy and a sham. We are too aware of our own weakness, too melancholy and insecure, too conscious of our illogicality and incoherence, too conscious of our faults; we have looked within ourselves for too long and seen too many things there. And so as we don't have authority we must invent another kind of relationship.

In these days, when a dialogue between parents and their children has become possible — possible though always difficult, always complicated by mutual prejudices, bashfulness, inhibitions — it is necessary that in this dialogue we show ourselves for what we are, imperfect, in the hope that our children will not resemble us but be stronger and better than us.

As we are all moved in one way or another by the problem of money, the first little virtue that it enters our heads to teach our children is thrift. We give them a moneybox and explain to them what a fine thing it is to save money instead of spending it, so that after a few months there will be lots of money, a nice little hoard of it; and how good it is not to give in to the wish to spend money so that in the end we can buy something really special. We remember that when we were children we were given a similar moneybox; but we forget that money, and a liking for saving it, were much less horrible and disgusting things when we were children than they are today; because the more time passes the more disgusting money becomes. And so the moneybox is our first mistake. We have installed a little virtue into our system of education.

That innocent-looking moneybox made of earthenware, in the shape of a pear or an apple, stays month after month in our children's room and they become used to its presence; they become used to the money saved inside it, money which in the dark and in secret grows like a seed in the womb of the earth; they like the money, at first innocently, as we like anything — plants and little animals for example — that grows because we take care of it; and all the time they long for that expensive something they saw in a shop window and which they will be able to buy, as we have explained to them, with the money they have saved up. When at last the moneybox is smashed and the money is spent, the children feel lonely and disappointed; there is no longer any money in their room, saved in the belly of the apple, and there isn't even the rosy apple any more; instead there is something longed for from a shop window, something whose importance and price we have made a great fuss about, but which, now that it is in their room, seems dull and plain and ordinary after so much waiting and so much money. The children do not blame money for this disappointment, but the object they have bought; because the money they have lost keeps all its alluring promise in their memories. The children ask for a new moneybox and for more money to save, and they give their thoughts and attention to money in a way that is harmful to them. They prefer money to things. It is not bad that they have suffered a disappointment; it is bad that they feel lonely without the company of money.

We should not teach them to save, we should accustom them to spending money. We should often give children a little money, small sums of no importance, and encourage them to spend it immediately and as they wish, to follow some momentary whim; the children will buy some small rubbishy toy which they will immediately forget as they will immediately forget money spent so quickly and thoughtlessly, and for which they have no liking. When they find the little rubbishy toy — which will soon break — in their hands they will be a bit disappointed but they will quickly forget the disappointment, the rubbishy toy and the money; in fact they will associate money with something momentary and silly, and they will think that money is silly, as it is right that they should think whilst they are children.

It is right that in the first years of their life children should live in ignorance of what money is. Sometimes this is impossible, if we are very poor; and sometimes it is difficult because we are very rich. All the same when we are very poor and money is strictly a matter of daily survival, a question of life or death, then it turns itself before the baby's eyes into food, coal or blankets so quickly that it is unable to harm his spirit. But if we are so-so, neither rich nor poor, it is not difficult to let a child live during its infancy unaware of what money is and unconcerned about it. And yet it is necessary, not too soon and not too late, to shatter this ignorance; and if we have economic difficulties it is necessary that our children, not too soon and not too late, become aware of this, just is it is right that they will at a certain point share our worries with us, the reasons for our happiness, our plans and everything that concerns the family's life together. And we should get them used to considering the family's money as something that belongs to us and to them equally, and not to us rather than to them; or on the other hand we can encourage them to be moderate and careful with the money they spend, and in this way the encouragement to be thrifty is no longer respect for a little virtue, it is not an abstract encouragement to respect something which is in itself not worth our respect, like money, rather it is a way of reminding the children that there isn't a lot of money in the house; it encourages them to think of themselves as adult and responsible for something that involves us as much as them, not something particularly beautiful or pleasant but serious, because it is connected with our daily needs. But not too soon and not too late; the secret of education lies in choosing the right time to do things.

Being moderate with oneself and generous with others; this is what is meant by having a just relationship with money, by being free as far as money is concerned. And there is no doubt that it is less difficult to educate a child so that he has such a sense of proportion, such a freedom, in a family in which money is earned and immediately spent, in which it flows like clear spring water and practically does not exist as money. Things become complicated where money exists and exists heavily, where it is a leaden stagnant pool that stinks and gives off vapours. The children are soon aware of the presence of this money in the family, this hidden power which no one ever mentions openly but to which the parents refer by means of complicated and mysterious names when they are talking among themselves with a leaden stillness in their eyes and a bitter curl to their lips; money which is not simply kept in a desk drawer but which accumulates who knows where and which can at any moment be sucked back into the earth, disappearing for ever and swallowing up both house and family. In families like this the children are constantly told to spend money grudgingly, every day the mother tells them to be careful and thrifty as she gives them a few coins for their tram fare; in their mother's gaze there is that leaden preoccupation and on her forehead there is that deep wrinkle which appears whenever money is discussed; there is the obscure fear that all the money will dissolve into nothing and that even those few coins might signify the first dust of a mortal and sudden collapse. The children in families like this often go to school in threadbare clothes and worn-out shoes and they have to pine for a long time, and sometimes in vain, for a bicycle or a camera, things which some of their friends who are certainly poorer than they are have had for quite a while. And then when they are given the bicycle they want the present is accompanied by severe orders not to damage it, not to lend such a magnificent object — which has cost a great deal of money — to anyone. In such a house admonitions to save money are constant and insistent — school books are usually bought second-hand, and exercise books at a cheap supermarket. This happens partly because the rich are often mean, and because they think they are poor, but above all because mothers in rich families are — more or less subconsciously — afraid of the consequences of money and try to protect their children by surrounding them with the lie of simple habits, even making them grow accustomed to little instances of privation. But there is no worse error than to make a child live in such a contradiction; everywhere in the house money talks its unmistakeable language; it is there in the china, in the furniture, in the heavy silverware, it is there in the comfortable journeys, in the luxurious summer holidays, in the doorman's greeting, in the servants' rituals; it is there in his parents' conversation, it is the wrinkle on his father's forehead, the leaden perplexity in his mother's gaze; money is everywhere, untouchable perhaps because it is so fragile, it is something he is not allowed to joke about, a sombre god to whom he can only turn in a whisper, and to honour this god, so as not to disturb its mournful immobility, he has to wear last year's overcoat that has got too small, learn his lessons from books that are in tatters and falling to pieces, and amuse himself with a country bumpkin's bicycle.

If we are rich and want to educate our children so that they have simple habits it must in that case be made very clear that all the money saved by following such simple habits is to be spent, without any hint of meanness, on other people. Such habits mean only that they are not greed or fear but a simplicity that has — in the midst of wealth — been freely chosen. A child from a rich family will not learn moderation because they have made him wear old clothes, or because they have made him eat a green apple for tea, or because they deny him a bicycle he has wanted for a long time; such moderation in the midst of wealth is pure fiction, and fictions always lead to bad habits. In this way he will only learn to be greedy and afraid of money. If we deny him a bicycle which he wants and which we could buy him we only prevent him from having something that it is reasonable a boy should have, we only make his childhood less happy in the name of an abstract principle and without any real justification. And we are tacitly saying to him that money is better than a bicycle; on the contrary he should learn that a bicycle is always better than money.

The true defence against wealth is not a fear of wealth — of its fragility and of the vicious consequences that it can bring — the true defence against wealth is an indifference to money. There is no better way to teach a child this indifference than to give him money to spend when there is money — because then he will learn to part with it without worrying about it or regretting it. But, it will be said, then the child will be used to having money and will not be able to do without it; if tomorrow he is not rich, what is he to do? But it is easier not to have money once we have learnt to spend it, once we have learnt how quickly it runs through our hands; and it is easier to learn to do without money when we are thoroughly familiar with it than when we have paid it the homage of our reverence and fear throughout our childhood, than when we have sensed its presence all around us and not been allowed to raise our eyes and look it in the face.

As soon as our children begin to go to school we promise them money as a reward if they do well in their lessons. This is a mistake. In this way we mix money — which is an ignoble thing — with learning and the pleasures of knowledge, which are admirable and worthy things. The money we give our children should be given for no reason; it should be given indifferently so that they will learn to receive it indifferently; but it should be given not so that they learn to love it, but so that they learn not to love it, so that they realize its true nature and its inability to satisfy our truest desires, which are those of the spirit. When we elevate money into a prize, a goal, an object to be striven for, we give it a position, an importance, a nobility, which it should not have in our children's eyes. We implicitly affirm the principle — a false one — that money is the crowning reward for work, its ultimate objective. Money should be thought of as a wage for work, not its ultimate objective but its wage — that is, its legitimate recognition; and it is clear that the scholastic work of children cannot have a wage. It is a small mistake — but a mistake — to offer our children money in return for domestic services, for doing little chores. It is a mistake because we are not our children's employers; the family's money is as much theirs as it is ours; those little services and chores should be done without reward, as a voluntary sharing in the family's life. And in general I think we should be very cautious about promising and providing rewards and punishments. Because life rarely has its rewards and punishments; usually sacrifices have no reward, and often evil deeds go unpunished, at times they are even richly rewarded with success and money. Therefore it is best that our children should know from infancy that good is not rewarded and that evil goes unpunished; yet they must love good and hate evil, and it is not possible to give any logical explanation for this.

We usually give a quite unwarranted importance to our children's scholastic performance. And this is nothing but a respect for the little virtue 'success'. It should be enough for us that they do not lag too far behind the others, that they do not fail their exams; but we are not content with this; we want success from them, we want them to satisfy our pride. If they do badly at school or simply not as well as we would wish, we immediately raise a barrier of nagging dissatisfaction between us and them; when we speak to them we assume the sulky, whining tone of someone complaining about an insult. And then our children become bored and distance themselves from us. Or we support them in their complaints that the teachers have not understood them and we pose as victims with them. And every day we correct their homework, and study their lessons with them. In fact school should be from the beginning the first battle which a child fights for himself, without us; from the beginning it should be clear that this is his battlefield and that we can give him only very slight and occasional help there. And if he suffers from injustice there or is misunderstood it is necessary to let him see that there is nothing strange about this, because in life we have to expect to be constantly misunderstood and misinterpreted, and to be victims of injustice; and the only thing that matters is that we do not commit injustices ourselves. We share the successes and failures of our children because we love them, but just as much and in the same way that they, little by little as they grow up, share our successes and failures, our joys and anxieties. It is not true that they have a duty to do well at school for our sake and to give the best of their skills to studying. Once we have started them in their lessons, their duty is simply to go forward. If they wish to spend the best of their skills on things outside school — collecting

Coleoptera or learning Turkish — that is their business and we have no right to reproach them, or to show that our pride has been hurt or that we feel dissatisfied with them. If at the moment the best of their skills do not seem to be applied to anything, then we do not have the right to shout at them very much in that case either; who knows, perhaps what seems laziness to us is really a kind of daydreaming and thoughtfulness that will bear fruit tomorrow. If it seems they are wasting the best of their energies and skills lying on the sofa reading ridiculous novels or charging around a football pitch, then again we cannot know whether this is really a waste of energy and skill or whether tomorrow this too will bear fruit in some way that we have not yet suspected. Because there are an infinite number of possibilities open to the spirit. But we, the parents, must not let ourselves be seized by a terror of failure. Our remonstrances must be like a squall of wind or a sudden storm — violent, but quickly forgotten — and not anything that could upset the nature of our relationship with our children, that could muddy its clarity and peace. We are there to console our children if they are hurt by failure; we are there to give them courage if they are humiliated by failure. We are also there to bring them down a peg or two when success has made them too pleased with themselves. We are there to reduce school to its narrow, humble limits; it is not something that can mortgage their future, it is simply a display of offered tools, from which it is perhaps possible to choose one which will be useful tomorrow.

What we must remember above all in the education of our children is that their love of life should never weaken. This love can take different forms, and sometimes a listless, solitary, bashful child is not lacking in a love of life, he is not overwhelmed by a fear of life, he is simply in a state of expectancy, intent on preparing himself for his vocation. And what is a human being's vocation but the highest expression of his love of life? And so we must wait, next to him, while his vocation awakens and takes shape. His behaviour can be like that of a mole, or of a lizard that holds itself still and pretends to be dead but in reality it has detected the insect that is its prey and is watching its movements, and then suddenly springs forward. Next to him, but in silence and a little aloof from him, we must wait for this leap of his spirit. We should not demand anything; we should not ask or hope that he is a genius or an artist or a hero or a saint; and yet we must be ready for everything; our waiting and our patience must compass both the possibility of the highest and the most ordinary of fates.

A vocation, an ardent and exclusive passion for something in which there is no prospect of money, the consciousness of being able to do something better than others, and being able to love this thing more than anything else — this is the only, the unique way in which a rich child can completely escape being conditioned by money, so that he is free of its claims; so that he feels neither the pride nor the shame of wealth when he is with others. He will not even be conscious of what clothes he is wearing, or of the clothes around him, and tomorrow he will be equal to any privation because the one hunger and thirst within him will be his own passion which will have devoured everything futile and provisional and divested him of every habit learnt in childhood, and which alone will rule his spirit. A vocation is man's one true wealth and salvation.

What chance do we have of awakening and stimulating in our children the birth and development of a vocation? We do not have much; however there is one way open to us. The birth and development of a vocation needs space, space and silence, the free silence of space. Our relationship with our children should be a living exchange of thoughts and feelings, but it should also include deep areas of silence: it should be an intimate relationship but it must not violently intrude on their privacy; it should be a just balance between silence and words. We must be important to our children and yet not too important; they must like us a little, and yet not like us too much — so that it does not enter their heads to become identical to us, to copy us and the vocation we follow, to seek our likeness in the friends they choose throughout their lives. We must have a friendly relationship with them, and yet we must not be too friendly with them otherwise it will be difficult for them to have real friends with whom they can discuss things they do not mention to us. It is necessary that their search for friends, their love-life, their religious life, their search for a vocation, be surrounded by silence and shadows, so that they can develop separately from us. But then, it will be said, our intimacy with our children has been reduced to very little. But in our relationships with them all these things — their religious life, their intellectual life, their emotional life, their judgement of other human beings — should be included as it were in summary form; for them we should be a simple point of departure, we should offer them the springboard from which they make their leap. And we must be there to help them, if help should be necessary; they must realize that they do not belong to us, but that we belong to them, that we are always available, present in the next room, ready to answer every possible question and demand as far as we know how to.

And if we ourselves have a vocation, if we have not betrayed it, if over the years we have continued to love it, to serve it passionately, we are able to keep all sense of ownership out of our love for our children. But if on the other hand we do not have a vocation, or if we have abandoned it or betrayed it out of cynicism or a fear of life, or because of mistaken parental love, or because of some little virtue that exists within us, then we cling to our children as a shipwrecked mariner clings to a tree trunk; we eagerly demand that they give us back everything we have given them, that they be absolutely and inescapably what we wish them to be, that they get out of life everything we have missed; we end up asking them for all the things which can only be given to us by our own vocation; we want them to be entirely our creation, as if having once created them we could continue to create them throughout their whole lives. We want them to be entirely our creation, as if we were not dealing with human beings but with products of the spirit. But if we have a vocation, if we have not denied or betrayed it, then we can let them develop quietly and away from us, surrounded by the shadows and space that the development of a vocation, the development of an existence, needs. This is perhaps the one real chance we have of giving them some kind of help in their search for a vocation — to have a vocation ourselves, to know it, to love it and serve it passionately; because love of life begets a love of life.

CPSIA information can be obtained
at www.ICGtesting.com
Printed in the USA
LVHW021654021221
705096LV00015B/1602